THE FALSE DOOR
BETWEEN LIFE AND DEATH

OTHER BOOKS BY TORIN M. FINSER

Education for Nonviolence
The Waldorf Way

Finding Your Self
Exercises and Suggestions to Support the Inner Life of the Teacher

Guided Self-Study
Rudolf Steiner's Path of Spiritual Development
A Spiritual-Scientific Workbook

In Search of Ethical Leadership
If not now, when?

Initiative
A Rosicrucian Path of Leadership

Leadership Development
Change from the Inside Out

Organizational Integrity
How to Apply the Wisdom of the Body
to Develop Healthy Organizations

Parables

Renovación escolar
Un viaje espiritual hacia el cambio
(translation of School Renewal)

School as a Journey
The Eight-Year Odyssey of a Waldorf Teacher and His Class

School Renewal
A Spiritual Journey for Change

A Second Classroom
Parent-Teacher Relationships in a Waldorf School

Silence Is Complicity
A Call to Let Teachers Improve Our Schools
through Action Research—Not NCLB

THE FALSE DOOR
BETWEEN LIFE AND DEATH

Supporting Grieving
Students, Teachers & Parents

TORIN M. FINSER, PHD

SteinerBooks | 2019

SteinerBooks
An imprint of Anthroposophic Press, Inc.
402 Union Street No. 58, Hudson, NY 12534
www.steinerbooks.org

Copyright © 2019 by Torin M. Finser.

All rights reserved. No part of this book may be reproduced, stored in a retrieval system, or transmitted in any form or by any means, electronic, mechanical, photocopying, recording, or otherwise, without the written permission of SteinerBooks. Excerpts by Rudolf Steiner have been edited for this book. They were previously published and copyrighted by SteinerBooks/Anthroposophic Press. Please see the bibliography for those books.

Cover image: *False Door of the Royal Sealer Neferiu,* ca. 2150–2010 BC (Metropolitan Museum of Art, New York)
Design: Jens Jensen

Excerpted texts used by permission:

Dan Lindholm, *The Death of Baldur*
(tr. E. and S. Berlin)

Herbert Hahn, *Das Goldene Kastchen*

(The Golden Casket; tr. T. Finser)

Library of Congress Control Number: 2019935131

ISBN: 978-1-62148-244-4 (paperback)
ISBN: 978-1-62148-245-1 (eBook)

Contents

Preface: The False Door ... ix
1. Personal Experiences of Death ... 1
2. When a Child Dies ... 9
3. Talking with Children about Death ... 15
4. One Day at a Time ... 20
5. Children and Grief ... 21
6. Spiritual Perspectives on Death ... 39
7. The Legend of Baldur ... 44
8. The Golden Casket ... 56
9. More Stories that Help Children with Loss ... 63
10. Adolescent Boys and Death ... 82
11. The Open Door (by Karine Munk Finser) ... 85
12. How to Stay Connected ... 90
13. Conclusion ... 98

Appendices:
    1. Verses for the Dead ... 101
    2. Mistletoe ... 106
    3. "The Juniper Tree" by the Grimm brothers ... 110
    4. "The Odor of Chrysanthemums" by D. H. Lawrence ... 118
    5. When a World Tragedy Comes into a Child or Teen's World ... 139
    6. Bringing Death Home ... 145

Bibliography ... 151

Dedication

*To my Mom
and all those helping us
from the other side*

Acknowledgements

I want to thank my loyal and talented research assistant Katlyn Boucher for her year of work on this project. I am also ever so grateful to Melissa Merkling for her wonderful perspective and expert editing of the text, and to Gene Gollogly and friends at SteinerBooks for continuing to support me as an author.

Preface
The False Door

> *"Death is not real, even in the relative sense—it is but birth to a new life—and you shall go on, and on, to higher and still higher planes of life, for aeons upon aeons of time. The universe is your home, and you shall explore its farthest recesses before the end of time. You are dwelling in the infinite mind of THE ALL, and your possibilities and opportunities are infinite, both in time and space. And at the end of the grand cycle of aeons, when THE ALL shall draw back into itself all of its creations—you will go gladly for you will then be able to know the whole truth of being at one with THE ALL."*
>
> **Three Initiates,** *The Kybalion: A Study of the Hermetic Philosophy of Ancient Egypt and Greece*

Perhaps more than any other culture, the ancient Egyptians knew that the physical body was temporary and would eventually fail and die. Thus they looked for a life beyond death, indeed spent much of life preparing for death. They recognized the nonphysical aspect of the human being, the *ba*, the soul-like quality that belonged to an individual human, inhabiting the physical body for a while and then returning to independent existence after death. Both the physical body and the *ba* were animated by the *ka*, a spiritual force derived directly from the Creator. To attain a successful afterlife, the *ba* had to be reunited with the *ka*. Then an individuality could live forever in a spiritual form known as the *ash*, the "effective being" or in other cultures, the eternal being (Faulkner, p. 11).

It was crucial for the deceased to make a successful transition from death to the life after as *ash*, and the many rituals, as well as the *Egyptian Book of the Dead*, are dedicated to the eternal life of the spirit. The vision of the afterlife was a source of comfort for the ancient Egyptians, as a time when they could look forward to an existence free of cold, hunger, and all the trials of everyday life on Earth. For those who could afford to build tombs to mark the importance of the transition, even though many lived daily lives in simple mud houses, the tombs were often made with great effort from stone. Although they could expect to live a relatively short time on the Earth (the average lifespan is thought to have been about 40 years), they planned their tombs as an eternal residence.

The deceased's body would be interned in the burial chamber below ground, along with objects that might be needed in the afterlife. That chamber was inaccessible to those still alive. Above that chamber was a public space or chapel where offerings could be made to the spirit and where friends and family could gather for special occasions. "The focal point of the chapel is a niched recess known as a 'false door,' through which the spirit could leave or enter the burial chamber; some false doors depict the spirit emerging to receive offerings" (ibid., p. 12).

Today we enter our own house after work to rest and sleep, just as the Egyptians believed that the spirit would enter the burial chamber to rejoin its mummified body at night and then reawake in the morning to go forth into the world—a process that was considered critical to one's afterlife. Sunrise and sunset were seen as a kind of birth and death; one's journey through the night was essential for returning to life each morning. This life-giving quality was the result of the nightly reunion with Osiris. Thus, passage through the false door had much to do with the renewing and life-giving power of Osiris, who ruled over the planting of crops (birth) and the harvest (death) that nourishes humankind. "In the middle of its nightly journey through the *Duat*, the dead sun would encounter Osiris, merge with the god, and through this union receive the power to come to life again and rise into the world at dawn" (ibid., p. 14).

Thus the picture of the false door indicates more than meets the eye. It represents the threshold between life and death.

Preface: The False Door

At the end of my book *A Second Classroom,* I shared a few observations on the door as a passage between the community and the inner life of a school. In the context of this book, I see the "false door" as a symbol of the larger dimensions of the human being on the journey to connect the living and the dead. From the perspective of everyday life on the Earth, we think of doors as real objects made of wood or metal. Yet from the perspective of the spiritual world, those doors are mere illusions given to our senses and our need for tactile experiences during physical life. One could say that the "false door" of the Egyptians is the real door, one that opens into the entire dimension of the spiritual world and the life of eternity beyond death.

This book is intended as an invitation to walk through the false door to find new connections to those who have gone before us.

Ever since I began working on my book *Education for Nonviolence,* I have had more and more requests to speak on issues surrounding death, especially in school communities. Likewise, my local newspaper, *The Keene Sentinel,* increasingly features stories depicting some aspect of the ongoing opioid crisis. In its obituaries there are now many that describe a young person, and even though the cause of death is often not mentioned it is clear something has changed. Then there are the cases of suicide, which do not receive as much attention in the media, although I have received heartbreaking accounts that cannot be included in this book. All in all, we face an issue that deserves our attention.

My hope is that this book will further the conversations we need to have about how we can pass through the door of death more gracefully to bring renewed life to our communities while expanding our connections to the larger community of those who have already crossed the threshold.

I

Personal Experiences of Death

The *Rückschau*, a daily review recommended by Rudolf Steiner, is a potent tool for inner development. As practiced by many students of Anthroposophy, it involves going backward through the events of the day as a preparation before sleep. Rather than reliving or reengaging in the drama of life, we are encouraged to let the pictures pass before our mind's eye, allowing the "photos" of the day play in reverse as a kind of tableau. Going backward is not always easy, but one tries to work gradually toward the very first moments of the day. This exercise helps us prepare for sleep, in that we have taken up one of the essential tasks of "digestion" inherent to the early stages of sleep. One can then enter the night with a sense of inner placement and rest.

As part of my preparation for writing this book, I have tried on occasion to do the same with my personal experiences of death, although going from earliest to latest in this case. It has been informative on many levels, and I suspect most people have a narrative of sorts when it comes to losing friends and loved ones. When the occasion is suitable, it is helpful to share such experiences, not only for the healing that comes by sharing but also to keep the soul alive to the connections that continue with those who have crossed.

In sharing the few instances that follow, I am mindful of how much of the real story remains untold, and how inadequate words are to describe momentous experiences. It is a bit like looking at an autumn leaf and trying to describe the tree. A leaf can give us only hints of the true existence of the tree as a whole. Nevertheless, we have to work with the materials we are given.

The following offers a few personal instances that have helped educate me in my growing relationship with those who have died.

My Grandmother

At the age of thirteen, I sat at the bedside of my grandmother as she prepared for death. She was able to speak and remain conscious until only a short time before the end, something that must have meant a lot to her as a lifelong speech artist and seeker of all things spiritual. I can vividly recall sitting to the right of her bed one day when she gave me a dark-blue book of poems by Henry Wadsworth Longfellow. Well used even then, the little volume has grown fragile with the passage of time. As I open the cover I can read her simple inscription, "For Torin from Nani, Christmas 1968."

She asked me to turn to page 280 and read the beginning of Longfellow's epic poem *Evangeline:* "This is the forest primeval. The murmuring pines and the hemlocks,/Bearded with moss, and in garments green, indistinct in the twilight./Stand like Druids of eld, with voices sad and prophetic,/Stand like harpers hoar, with beards that rest on their bosoms..." Then she became the speech teacher, asking me to read it again with true hexameter, long, short short, long, short short.... She showed me how to live into the pictures, to see those images while I was reading. She was never satisfied, and I felt inadequate. Yet, after a while, she was tired and suggested I continue to practice on my own.

I have been doing this throughout my life. That book traveled with me, and in moments of trial I have often returned to her favorite *Evangeline,* the story of love and faithfulness, heartbreak and service. During childhood family vacations in Nova Scotia, I had a chance to see some of the pines and hemlocks, often "bearded with moss and in garments green" hanging from the branches. Years later, I attended Bowdoin College, Longfellow's alma mater, and spent much time in the library (named after him) with some of his originals. Then, a few years later, when teaching seventh grade and relating the story of early explorations of the Maritimes, I led my class in reciting portions of *Evangeline.* Again, I felt inadequate. So much was living in me, and so little could find expression in the actual words spoken by those seventh graders (my first group).

Through my experience with Grandmother Nani, I have found that those who cross over remain with us, especially when we speak and occupy ourselves with poems and texts with which they had been connected. Holding the book in my hands is an entry point, but the real work is in the thought content and the spiritual striving with the material. With each passing year I feel a stronger flow of support and encouragement from Nani. Her embrace is loving and strong.

My Class Teacher

Ruth Eastman was my class teacher for eight years, a stretch that began and ended in unusual ways. My original teacher died after a few days of teaching us in first grade, and so Mrs. Eastman was asked to step in. She had recently lost her husband after serving in his dental practice for many years. She was a student of Anthroposophy but had no formal Waldorf teacher training. Her age was unknown to her students, but it was clear she was by far the oldest teacher in the building.

Nonetheless, she made up for her lack of training with extra effort. There were times that we had glimpses of that fact, such as when she alluded to doing multiple watercolor paintings at home before getting it right or having to stay late at the library researching a new theme. She was also tone deaf, so when it came time for us to practice our recorders, she relied on what the music teacher had introduced and sat at her desk, listening patiently as we practiced. Then, the strangest thing happened: Her listening was so intense and her posture so supportive (rather than correcting papers while we played our instruments) that we focused and held together even without her overt direction. In later years, our class was almost always selected to play our instruments at assemblies—the group with a tone-deaf teacher!

Mrs. Eastman loved literature, and the way she held a book will always be with me. She would hold a book with utmost reverence and gently turn each page with a look of curiosity on her face. She brought us many wonderful stories in those early years, and later on she often read to us during lunch hour. In fact, one of my favorite books was *The King of Ireland's Son* by Padraic Colum—and wouldn't you know, while looking through my shelves recently for something else, I found that book, a very old edition, bearing an inscription from Mrs. Eastman.

She died soon after our class graduated. I was not present for her passing, nor was I there for my eighth-grade graduation, as my father was transferred to Brussels a few months before the eight-year journey with my friends ended. Thus was the unusual beginning and ending of my Waldorf cycles.

Yet I did see Ruth Eastman once more in the Fellowship Community before she died. It was a brief exchange, and much of the luster of the former class teacher had faded. I came away feeling that she had given all her life forces to the class and was now just waiting for the end.

I have learned much from Mrs. Eastman in the years since her passing. One lesson has to do with the interplay of outer skills and inner striving. When hiring teachers, it is best of course to select those who have had formal teacher training and have developed their skills in the art of teaching—parents can be unforgiving of serious deficiencies. Nonetheless, looking back at my time with Mrs. Eastman and countless other teachers, it was not their skillfulness that stayed with me most, but rather their liveliness as individuals, their capacity to model learning, and their striving as human beings.

Mrs. Eastman would probably never be hired by a school today (twenty years as a dental assistant requires different skills), yet she did so much for us and continues to "vote" for me from the other side. When I struggle with a new subject or find myself in unfamiliar terrain, I turn to her for help. She is still my class teacher.

Passing of a Child

Some years later, the sister of one of my students died of cancer while I was a class teacher myself. I was able to experience the struggles and gradual passing through the eyes of another child—the times when conversation was needed and times when the worst thing would have been to raise the topic. The whole school community became involved, and the loss of a cherished child at a young age was deeply tragic.

As a school, we had some time to prepare, and I began casting about for ways we could work with the children once the last stage was crossed. It was then that I found a story in German by Herbert Hahn, one of the original teachers at the first Waldorf school in Stuttgart. As far as I knew, "The Golden Casket" has not been translated, so as part of my inner preparation I began the slow process of rendering the story in English. By the time my student's sister died, I had gotten to the stage at which the story lived in me, not in polished form but well enough to tell it in public.

So the day after her death, we had an assembly, and at my suggestion we invited the older grades and high school in first. I told them they would hear a story, but urged them to listen to the larger metaphor and bring their ideas back to the classroom to discuss in subsequent days with their teachers. One of our gifted subject teachers played music as the younger children came into the assembly hall. When everyone was settled in, I told "The Golden Casket." There was a hush in the room, and then everyone filed out, accompanied by music.

In the days that followed, teachers and parents had the most remarkable things to share. Some children did not say a word that night, or even the next day. Some made seemingly casual remarks; others wanted to tell the story. Most saw the connection between the story and the passing of their friend. Even weeks later, we heard observations that showed how deeply the themes of "The Golden Casket" were working in the soul life of many children.

It is for this reason that I include the entire story as a separate chapter of this book. The reader can work with it as needed.

Passing of a Colleague

William Ward was a true Renaissance individual, one of the most versatile class teachers I have ever known. Along with Arnold Logan, he put on massive musical productions at a nearby Waldorf school. They involved practically every child and student in grades 1 to 12. After many years of successful teaching, William was diagnosed with a brain tumor.

I was fortunate to see him a few weeks before his passing. He stood in his living room and made a small gesture, cupping his hands and then spreading them far out on either side, saying, "The things we are concerned with on a daily basis are so small, but the spiritual world is *so large!*" He was optimistic even when in pain, and he also left us his wonderful book, *Traveling Light: Walking the Cancer Path.*

My Father-in-Law

We all attended Nikolai and Naja's wedding in Dublin, and the following day my wife Karine and I took her parents out for supper at a nearby restaurant. I vividly remember Mofa (Karine's father Jørn Jensen) sitting across the table from us, with his right arm looped over the back of his wife's chair. He had been tired all day, but he still wore a wonderful smile and spoke of his love for his wife Lise and their many years of marriage. We talked about many things, some quite inconsequential, and I never imagined this would be the last time we saw him. A week later he was gone.

Karine and I visited his body in the basement of the hospital in Ronne, where he had died the previous day. It was the same physical person, but it was clear that the *real* person—the light we had seen in the restaurant just a week earlier—was gone. He lay so still, and we stood there in grief and shock, contemplating this unexpected passage through the door of death. We said a prayer, Karine sang, and we departed to prepare for the funeral.

I had some time to myself while the immediate family spent the next couple of days making the many necessary arrangements. Fortunately, I had brought along a copy of Rudolf Steiner's *Life between Death and Rebirth*, so I read to Mofa for several hours each day. It was then that I had a remarkable experience—it was as if his presence grew, and I could feel his gratitude. Between readings and walks, I stopped at the other house to check in with the others and their preparations, and it seemed he was less present there than when I was reading. It occurred to me that the things so many people fuss over—the type of flowers, the sequence of the funeral program, who would carry the coffin, and so on—all seemed to be about those left behind and not the one who had crossed.

How much of our daily activity is about the "small things" in life? Why do we give them so much space? If we could simply take the perspective of the ones who have crossed, we might reallocate our time and energy in ways we have not yet imagined—recognizing the wide expanse represented by William Ward's outstretched arms.

My Mother

There is so much I could relate about my dear mother, and much is still in process within me, so I will select only a couple of scenes from her passing.

I arrived at her home in Mill Valley in the evening to find most of her extended family around her hospital bed, which had been placed in the center of her living room. My father, brother, his children and mine, and my sister were all there. My mother was happy to be surrounded by those she loved, and fortunately for us she could still speak. I sat on one side of her bed with my brother, my sister hovered near her head (occasionally administering some morphine), and my father sat on her other side. She was intent on holding all our hands.... Then she asked that we take out the family photo albums and asked us to remember together. She asked, "Where is the picture of our vacation in Sandy Hook, New Jersey?" At the time it seemed less important to me. Later, however, I realized that, like so much else in her life, she was doing this for us. She was telling us that we had many good memories to hold onto, even after her death.

That was her last night and she passed early the next morning. We all worked together in forming the three-day wake in which much was shared and experienced as a family. We had a simple service in her living room (I played recorder) and then we went to the crematorium, which represents the second scene I wish to share; the building was gray concrete, heavy and very depressing, the scene inside was drab, and with just a few more words and a recitation, we placed the casket on the conveyor belt and saw it disappear into the furnace.

We left the building very sad, and began to climb into our respective cars in the parking lot. Suddenly somebody shouted, "Look, look!" My first reaction was "What now," but we all got out of our cars again and looked up into the sky. There we saw the tall chimney of the crematorium, and from the top rose a long, fiery column of flame and then a huge tower of smoke that reached all the way up into the clouds. It was our Oma, my mother, rising to the heavens. We stood there in silence, and as we watched our mood lifted. We were okay because she was okay. She was letting go of all things earthly and returning to her spiritual home.

As I sit and write these few lines, I glance up every now and then and see a picture of my Mom holding me as a baby, her round golden clock, a photo of the Goetheanum, and a handwritten verse my mother had given me many years before:

> Quiet I bear within me
> I bear within myself
> Forces to make me strong.
> Now will I be imbued
> With their glowing warmth.
> Now will I fill myself
> With my own will's resolve.
> And I will feel the quiet
> Pouring through all my being.
> When by my steadfast striving
> I become strong
> To find within myself
> The source of strength,
> The strength of inner quiet.

I say this verse every morning since her death.

2

When a Child Dies

At the Death of a Child I
And the child's soul
Was lent to us
According to thy Will
Out of spirit worlds.
And the child's soul was led back to Thee
According to Thy will
Into spirit worlds.
        Rudolf Steiner (adapted by R. Lewis)

While Rudolf Steiner was lecturing at the Goetheanum, a young boy, Theo Faiss, was killed by a vehicle that had overturned. It was a death that shocked the community and elicited deeply felt responses. Steiner said at the time that what Theo took was a path of sacrifice orchestrated by the spiritual world: "A family moves into the neighborhood of the building. This family has a child whose soul nature is especially gifted, and he sacrifices his etheric body to envelop the building in its forces." The child's body of formative forces is a "gift from the spiritual world." Its power protects the building. "There is something wonderfully powerful at work in such connection" (Selg, p. 56).

Each child is a gift from the spiritual world, but a child that dies an untimely death is doubly so. Those children make themselves available through sacrifice, and their life forces strengthen and protect those who have been left behind.

In this light, I have reviewed stories of children who have died, particularly in the context of a school. They are truly remarkable. Again and again, the passing evokes latent qualities in others; people find connections to their spiritual roots, to God, and to one another.

One cannot do justice to the many such instances, but what emerges from hearing these stories is a sense of how the entire community is often reborn. There is usually no script or protocol to follow when tragedy strikes, so there is often a spontaneous, creative process that unfolds in the days between the death and the funeral. People come together in new ways, find meaningful ways to share their grief and remember, and rituals are born in the moment. This is a kind of applied spirituality that our world needs; it is fresh and self-generated.

Old rituals still have a place in the world and are a source of comfort for many, but we also need to create new rituals, to apply our spiritual insights in the moment, in real situations. There is nothing more immediate than the sudden death of a child in a school community. All that we can theorize and conceptualize has to be put aside as one grapples with a real situation.

My wife and I were at a ski resort some years ago while our son Ionas was out doing runs on the slopes with his friends. One of the mothers, a dear friend and colleague, joined us at our table to chat about our school and our children (she had two girls, one by then a teenage driver). It all seemed to be a normal day in parenting land. We parted happily, but when Karine and I returned home we received a tragic phone call: Just a short time earlier, that sweet teen, with all the promise of a life ahead of her, had been hit by an eighteen-wheeler at an intersection near home.

In the hours that followed, we cried, comforted, made calls, and in those first halting steps, set up a place in the home for remembrance. Visiting the funeral home the next day, attending the funeral, living "along with" the grieving family—what a journey. Words are inadequate. But to this day, when our paths cross with the mother, there is a connection that is very alive. Her daughter brought us together, as she did with many others.

I could speak of the child who fell from a tree on the school playground or of others who succumbed to cancer. Each story is unique and speaks to more than the sweet one who lost a life. I have interviewed teachers and parents and collected tips to pass on. However, most of all we need to hear the voices of those who have been through the process, for they speak of a wisdom that lies deeper than the granite of New Hampshire.

Earlier I highlighted themes of sacrifice, protection, and community development in the context of a child's death, but as we continue to press against the "false door," I would like to probe a bit deeper into the recesses beyond. It seems to me there is something especially significant for our time in connection with the mystery of death.

When a child is born these days, it has to adapt not only to a new family and friends, but also to an entirely different age. Imagine, just a hundred years ago there were no electronic devices, no commercial airplanes, no pre-packaged frozen food. Much has changed in a relatively short period of time, and it is hard to imagine all the adjustments a child has to make when beginning a new journey on this Earth. In fact, we know from spiritual science that the time spent between two incarnations corresponds to the period of change in the cultural life on the Earth. People tend to return only when there is virtually no similarity to the conditions when they last came to Earth (Steiner, 1968, p. 27).

An early death leads to a more rapid return to the Earth, for there is less to work through. Thus we come to Rudolf Steiner's remarkable observation that when we die, regardless of one's age, we need to shed the years accumulated on the Earth. In the journey after death, we go gradually from being old to being young again (the reverse of what happens with our life on Earth!). "To begin with, we carry the errors and shortcomings of earthly life into the spiritual world. Then gradually, during cosmic existence, they are removed" (ibid., p. 29). On Earth we grow old, whereas we grow younger in the spiritual world.

It is not until the age of thirty-five that we have experienced more-or-less consciously all that is needed from earlier phases of human existence. This means that an early death brings about a more rapid condition of "sleep" between death and rebirth. So when a child dies, many of the life forces that would have been devoted to living a normal biography are instead released back to the universe. They are then available for others and for the progress of humanity. Thus, in a very real sense, one can say that the death of a child is a sacrifice.

All around us, we are being called upon to develop greater consciousness—global warming, school violence, the opioid epidemic, and so on. In all these cases, the human being is on center stage. We are the decisive element as to whether things tip one way or the other; continued descent into the abyss or reclaiming balance. In each case, it is our consciousness and subsequent actions that will be crucial. Will we awake to the challenge or try to postpone or sidestep the issues with additional politics and rhetoric?

In the novel *The President is Missing,* coauthored with James Patterson, Bill Clinton writes:

> Participation in our democracy seems to be driven by the instant-gratification worlds of Twitter, Snapchat, Facebook, and the twenty-four-hour news cycle. We're using modern technology to revert to primitive kinds of human relations. The media knows what sells—conflict and division. It's also quick and easy. All too often, anger works better than answers; resentment better than reason; emotion trumps evidence. (Clinton and Patterson, p. 59)

In this sea of false equivalency and distortion, we are losing our humanity. It is hard to imagine what it must like to be a child in today's world. It is an act of courage!

Waldorf parents and teachers often speak of the preservation of childhood. We try to create safe havens in which children are still allowed to play and where imagination means more than the latest Nintendo game, while classrooms radiate with color and projects created by the students. This is clear to anyone who has visited a Waldorf school.

But I would like to turn this equation around 180 degrees. I feel that in a world that many adults have messed up, it is our children who are there to protect us! Through their simple yet honest way of seeing the world, through their wonderful sense for the obvious, and their belief in the goodness of others, they are setting an example that the rest of us need to notice. Their innocence (like that of the Norse god Baldur, whose story follows in another chapter) is both vulnerable and shining.

Rudolf Steiner often spoke of a fourfold aspect to the human being: the physical body; our life force (etheric). which stays with us from birth to death; our consciousness (astral); and an "I," or self. We know of the assaults on the physical, and many have made great progress in eating nutritious foods and caring for the body with exercise, and so on. Those who have worked to change their habits such as quitting smoking know what a challenge it can be to change aspects of our etheric. However, it is our astral body that is especially under attack today through the bombardment of our senses by distractions and our inability to really think or remember, all of which are symptoms that have led in part to the social and political manifestations we see all around us. Polarization is an affliction of consciousness.

This is where children come into the picture. Every so often they are wonderfully "whole." They see the forest for the trees, and they can be wise and yet spontaneous. They are, in short, the antidote to much of what is happening in the world today. We all need to follow our children more, heeding their way of seeing the world and their joy in discovery.

Having said this, we can turn to the theme of this chapter, "When a Child Dies." Some react with "shock," appalled at what is happening and running for an exit. This is more than a comment on teen suicides and the opioid crisis; it is a condition we face together as human beings. Unless we make our planet more child-friendly, we may not (as the African myth in another chapter relates) have more children.

Rudolf Steiner tells us that the constant attacks on our fourfold constitution are impairing our ability to function. This can be addressed through successive incarnations, through many cycles of life and death, destruction and renewal (Steiner, 1968, p. 37). Children who die early help us as adults when have failed to help ourselves.

The loss of childhood is larger than any single school shooting, no matter how tragic each instance is in the lives of families and loved ones. The loss described in this chapter has to do with the depletion of life forces (the etheric). which has plagued so many today and shows up in ever greater susceptibility to a host of attacks on the immune system and other illnesses. Children have been robbed of free playtime at school, as well as many of the arts that nourish emotional intelligence and downtime that replenishes their life forces. As stated at the end of my book *Education for Nonviolence*, we need a Bill of Rights for Children, a pledge to address the loss of childhood in our hectic world.

3

Talking with Children about Death

In Waldorf schools, the use of stories such as "The Golden Casket" and others is a potent tool for working with a group, as children will child will hear what they each need to hear. This has to do with the power of imagination and the inner compass that points us in the right direction. Painting, drama, music, and other arts also provide opportunities for working with grief. But there are times when one has to deal with an individual situation, one-on-one and in the moment. Teachers and parents need to act, and often there is little prior guidance for those rare situations when one has to speak about the loss of a sibling or parent.

To begin with, let's look at some well-formulated "do's and don'ts" from psychologists.

Do:

- Tell the truth right away about what happened. The truth gives an explanation for your own tears and pain. Being open and emotional can help your child learn how to mourn.
- Be prepared for a variety of emotional responses. Realize that no matter how you approach this subject your child might be upset, even angry, at the loss. *Accept* your child's emotional reactions. You will have time to address matters again after your child has had time to process the initial trauma.
- Make sure to use the words *dead* or *died*. Many find using these words uncomfortable, preferring instead to use terms such as *passed away, loss, crossed over,* or *asleep,* but research shows that using realistic descriptions of death helps the grieving process.

- Share information in doses. Gauge what your child can handle by giving information in small bits at a time. You'll know what more to do based on the questions your child asks.
- Be comfortable saying "I don't know." Having all the answers is never easy, especially during a time of such heartache. It's helpful to tell your child that you may not know about certain things, such as, "How did Grandpa die?" "What happens to Aunt Rita at the funeral home?" "What made Spike run into the street, Mommy?"...as well as other unanswerable questions.
- Cry. Cry together. Cry often. It's healthy and healing.
- Allow your child to participate in rituals. Let children pick clothing for your loved one, photos for the memorial, a song or spiritual reading. This will help them gain a sense of control of the traumatic loss.
- Let your child grieve in his or her own way. Allow your child to be silent about a death. It's also natural for children to feel lonely and isolate themselves at this time. It's common, too, for children to seem unaffected by the loss. There is no right way to grieve.
- Prepare your child for what she or he will see in the funeral home or service. Tell children what they will see, who will be there, how people may be feeling and what they will be doing. For young children, be specific in your descriptions of what the surroundings will look like. For example, describe the casket and clothes and that the body will be posed. Or if it's a memorial service, talk about where the body is, whether it's been cremated, placed in a closed coffin, or already been buried. Bring someone who can care for the child if you feel too distraught.
- Prepare your child for the future without your loved one. Talk about how it will feel to celebrate birthdays, anniversaries, holidays and special moments without your loved one. Ask your child to help plan how to move through the next calendar event.
- Prepare to talk about thoughts and feelings often. It is likely that you'll have to tend to the subject of death for days, weeks and

months to come. Check in and be available for ongoing discussions; *mourning is a process.*
- Remember to take care of yourself. As parents, we sometimes forget about taking care of ourselves during this time. Children learn what they see, so be a role model for self-care at this critical time.

Don't:

- Don't hide your grief from your child. Seeing you grieve during (and long after) your loved one's death will let the child know that it's normal and healthy to cry and feel sad after a significant loss.
- Don't be afraid to share memories of your loved one. Sometimes parents feel afraid to talk about the person who has died, thinking it will cause pain to others. Research shows that the pain of reliving memories or sharing stories actually aids in healing and closure.
- Don't avoid connecting with your child because you feel helpless or uncomfortable, or don't know what to say. Sometimes a knowing look can be a powerful connection. Even a touch or a hug can offer great comfort.
- Don't change the subject when your child comes into the room. Doing so places a mark of taboo on the subject of death. Instead, adjust your words and level of information while a child is present.
- Don't change your daily routine. Children need consistency. Try as much as possible to keep your usual daily routines at home and at work. Also, try to ensure that your child continues to take part in usual activities like school and social events.
- Don't think that death puts a ban on laughter. Laughter is a great healing tool. Being able to laugh about memories or moments with your loved one signals just how important their presence was in your life.
- Don't put a time limit on your child's bereavement—or your own. Everyone grieves in their own way. Recognize that a new normal will have to occur—and that time is needed to readjust to a significant death. If you need additional support, reach out to your

child's school, physician, or religious community. Professional help with a mental health therapist trained in bereavement can be sought as well.*

In *How Do We Tell the Children?* Dan Schaefer and Christine Lyons acknowledge the difficulty of telling a child about death, in part because it brings up issues for us, including our own mortality. Since many are not comfortable with the idea of death and hide behind euphemisms, it is doubly difficult to find the right words to tell children in terms they understand:

> "It wasn't enough to just explain how their father died," she told me. I had to learn to help them cope with their feelings of loss, and I had no way of knowing what was going on in their heads....
>
> Those parents who just say "He died" leave a lot to the child's imagination. What might other people have told him about what happened? And what might he have overheard? (Schaefer, pp. 8, 13)

Schaefer and Lyons go on to remind us of age-appropriateness and the importance of establishing trust through the process, which should include checking in afterward to see what has been assimilated and what needs further amplification. It is more than just sharing information. This is a crucial time for relationship building.

Above all, we need to overcome our reluctance to talk about death, one of the key motivations behind this book. Death, as has been discussed in other chapters, is part of a larger cycle:

> ...like leaves falling in autumn, it has touch, taste, sound, feeling, think about it...to be in a culture where death is not seen as failure or an enemy, it is seen as a stage of life.
>
> We are in a very interesting position in this culture. We are demographically an aging culture, with youth-oriented values, so more and more people, as they get older, are seen as "less valued" in our society. We value the latest interface with the internet, and there is no lineage passed down in a tradition, by older generations. (ibid., p. 14)

---

* See Deborah Serani PsyD, *Depression and Your Child*; also, https://www.psychologytoday.com/us/experts/deborah-serani-psyd.

Recently I attended a dinner with friends from our extended family who have spent much time in Mozambique working with communications and food issues in rural communities. They began the evening meal by taking a small glass and spilling some of the contents on the floor in remembrance of those who have passed before us. We were all asked to remember someone. It was a powerful moment. Within seconds the dimension of our consciousness became wider and deeper.

Later that same evening, we heard the story of a village that forgot to ask permission of its departed elders when making a technological improvement. When they went to throw the switch, it did not work. After much fiddling with the equipment, the village elder stepped forward and did the blessing, and then everything functioned smoothly.

Some might say there is no "evidence" that the blessing of the departed makes any difference, and the above is just an anecdotal story. Yet it is that kind of thinking that has landed us where we are today in world affairs. Reductionist, evidence-based logic has not solved many of the most pressing issues at hand. But the real lesson from the above glimpses into Mozambique is the importance of culture. Rituals such as pouring out a glass are part of traditions that can hold people together, give meaning, and provide inner strength. Fortune 500 companies often pay top dollar to do the same for their "team." Culture is important.

We need to foster a culture that supports death and grieving, a culture that reframes attitudes toward death and allows graceful passing. Death is not a failure or an ending; it is a transition, a false door.

As the Boomer generation ages, this quest will become increasingly urgent. As they have done with many other social issues over the past sixty or so years, the Baby Boomers can make a difference in questions of death. Often it begins close to home and in how we speak about death with others. As we struggle to understand and to find the words, we can come together to share experiences, and by sharing a new culture can arise.

4

ONE DAY AT A TIME

"There are two days of every week about which we should not worry; two days in which we should be kept free from fear and apprehension.

"One of these days is Yesterday, with its mistakes and cares, its faults and blunders, its aches and pains. Yesterday has passed forever beyond our control. All the money in the world cannot undo a single act performed; we cannot erase a single word said. Yesterday is Gone!

"The other day we should not worry about is Tomorrow with its possible burdens, its large promise and poor performance. Tomorrow is also beyond our immediate control. Tomorrow's sun will rise, either in splendor or behind a mask of clouds. But it will Rise. Until it does, we have no stake in tomorrow, for it is yet unborn.

"This leaves only one day... TODAY! Any man can fight the battle of just one day. It is only when you and I have the burdens in those two awful entities, Yesterday and Tomorrow, that we break down.

"It is not the experience of Today that drives men mad. It is the remorse or bitterness for something that happened Yesterday and the dread of what Tomorrow may bring. Let us, therefore, live but One Day at a Time."

RICHARD LEWIS (pp. 11–12)

5

Children and Grief

With the resources available online today, it is possible to connect with many organizations, both locally and nationally, that can provide support when there is a loss. There are many dedicated people who provide counseling for children, support groups and places to share with others with similar experiences. The Seasons for Growth Children and Young People's Program is one such example:

> The Children and Young People's Program uses a safe, engaging curriculum structure that incorporates a wide range of age-appropriate activities involving drawing, role play, stories, discussion, play-dough, music and journal activities.
>
> There are four different levels of the program. Each level includes eight weekly sessions, a final celebration session and two subsequent re-connector sessions (that range from 40 minutes to an hour, depending on age). Each weekly session explores a concept theme such as Life is like the Seasons, Change is Part of Life, Valuing My Story, Caring for my Feelings, Making Good Choices.
>
> All four levels of the program have the flexibility to cater to participants with different learning needs or preferences. The learning processes reflect a deep respect for children's capacity to cope, problem-solve, make good choices, set realistic goals and connect with others. Such learning develops best in supportive social contexts with peers and a caring, skilled adult 'Companion.' Children's learning is documented in a personal "Seasons for Growth" journal so that participants can re-visit their insights in the future.*

---

* See https://www.goodgrief.org.au/seasons-for-growth.

Many of these programs are peer-based, which can provide reciprocal social and emotional support. Many organizations offer formal and informal opportunities for peer relationship building and the self-healing that can come through sharing lived experiences in groups. Some provide a companion to help with a developmentally appropriate approach and sequence of activities and discussions. Companions model empathy, understanding and acceptance so that participants can become partners in learning. As the Seasons for Growth website states, "Research has shown that increasing protective factors, and minimizing risk factors (or taking steps to minimize their impact) can promote mental health and wellbeing in children and adults." The grieving process can strengthen social skills and a participant's sense of belonging, and give a renewed feeling of hope for living into the future.

In her insightful book, *Talking with Children about Loss*, Maria Trozzi describes some of the myths around children and grieving:

1. Death is not a part of living.
2. Children don't mourn.
3. We can protect children by shielding them from loss. (p. 6)

Shielding children from death can cause a repeat of the "loss cycle" in their future relationships and what Hope Edelman calls an "attachment/abandonment pattern" (ibid., p. 9). This means that many fail to develop feelings of security within their future relationships. Dr. Sandra Fox, who dedicated more than fifty years to helping children with a loss, outlined four tasks needed to help children who mourn: "*Understanding* what caused the loss, *grieving* or experiencing the painful feelings associated with the loss, *commemorating* the value of the loss, and *going on with life* by accepting and integrating the loss psychologically and emotionally within themselves" (ibid., p.10). With these tasks in mind, caregivers need to foster honest and open relationships with children. This includes providing a safe and secure space in which chilren can mourn and serve as models for mourning in healthy ways. As Rabbi Grollman said so eloquently, "Grief shared is grief diminished" (ibid., p. 11).

Trozzi cautions against using euphemisms and confusing language when we talk to children about death. If one says that Rover, the pet dog, was "put to sleep," a young child might fear that one night she might no longer wake up. "Passing away" or "passing over" are frequently used. When a child heard the phrase "We lost our Uncle Sam," she responded by saying, "Well, let's go find him" (ibid., p. 14). Children use imagination and "magical thinking" to cope with death, but sometimes that goes too far. "When I asked her what happened to Kevin, which is always the first question I ask to help children understand a loss, she told me that he died because 'he ate his dessert before his sandwich.'... Even adults can say things such as 'If only I had called my father, I could have stopped him from leaving so early in the morning, and he wouldn't have gotten killed in the accident'" (ibid., p. 18). Trozzi concludes that using the word *death* is okay, and that one can then go on to describe what that means in age-appropriate ways. But we should not try to deny or shield children completely from experiencing loss.

My colleague and friend, Kim John Payne, has done much work with parents and teachers through his bestselling book *Simplicity Parenting* and his training programs. He wrote an article titled "When a World Tragedy Comes into a Child or Teen's World." In it he describes how parents and caregivers can offer a reassuring and living presence in the days and weeks after a tragedy strikes. He describes how children especially can feel overwhelmed by events that they may not really understand, but catch wind of through news reports and adult conversations:

> Younger children may come to you for more information, explanations, clarifications, while older ones may need some gentle prompting to speak about what they have been hearing and seeing... this seeking to understand and integrate may take some time. This is an opportunity for parents and teachers to offer wisdom and loving presence, to meet each child in the way he or she needs to be met. Please consider the age of your child and how any of this information may impact him or her—as their parents you are the best expert on how to protect and strengthen your own children and your family. Regardless of their age one thing is constant: they need our reassurance that most people are good, that even in overwhelming disaster, there are always good people helping others in need. Our loving

presence and deep quiet listening may be more helpful than a lot of explanations. Children can, and do, work things out for themselves according to their own abilities, over time, in the warmth and calmness of adult presence.

However, if your child either has not directly experienced or heard about a terrible event or has not taken it in, it may be best to "let it be," knowing that when your child does want to speak about this, you will be ready. You may be wondering about your child having heard about this and not speaking about it. For the younger child we encourage you to watch your child's play very carefully. For the tween or teen, usually the signs to watch are more in their behavior and attitude. Both play and behavior may be a guide to what is going on inwardly for your child. (see appendix, page 143)

See the appendix for the full article.

Rev. Richard Lewis published a small book that touches on many aspects of death, including the spiritual contributions of those who die young. The following is his summary.

Spiritual Contributions of Those Who Have Died Young

> They give a tremendous surplus of pure life forces that can be used in terms of the angelic realm.
> They have brought many people close together; they have taught us more lessons than we could have imagined; their pure qualities of soul we can now look upon as colorations of soul, like a rainbow shining through a break in the clouds.
> In regard to materialistic souls in danger of being cut off from the spiritual world, their surplus is used to save souls who could not otherwise be saved.
> These forces work with the group of souls into which they were born and enhance their spirituality.
> They help incoming souls strongly to a better incarnation spiritually, by strengthening their spirit.
> Those dying young enter more rapidly and clearly into the spiritual world.
> Their forces strengthen the ideal life of humankind to see better the Earth as permeated by the spirit.
> They work for the good of humanity in general and set themselves universal tasks for the coming future (Lewis, p. 171).

What Advice Can You Give a School that Has Lost a Child?

Although this particular chapter is in the middle of the book, it is actually the section I had to write last. I even finished the conclusion before I could get myself to write this chapter. The reason for this has to do with the content, which arises from numerous interviews that took place over several months. These conversations were with parents, teachers and friends who had experienced a loss in their school community. It is near impossible to capture both the substance and the tone of what was shared.

Those who have lost a child have been through the worst tragedy life can bring. Speaking to those left behind was one of the most transformative experiences of my life. The mothers, fathers, teachers, partners and friends who suffered loss are remarkable people, modern-day saints. They have walked a path that words cannot adequately describe. At times in the interviews there were pregnant pauses, at times volumes were communicated with very few words. It was a deep honor to be brought into their world of grief. Even though in many cases the loss occurred years ago, the soul-space around the child's death was still very tender. As one mother stated, "The relationship has changed but did not end."

Thus I approach this chapter from two directions. First I want to capture some of the main points arising from this question: What advice can you give to a school community that has experienced the loss of a child? Next, I share first-hand accounts in their own words—one from a mother, one from a teacher (both connected to Waldorf schools), and then experiences collected by the National Education Association related to losses in public schools. My hope is that the reader will be encouraged to seek out those who have a loss in their biography and help them continue with a healing process that has become part of a life journey.

How Can a Community Work with the Loss of a Child?

Everyone I interviewed spoke about the importance of community gatherings. In some cases, they gathered together right away so that "we could cry together." In other instances the community gathered a day or two later, sometimes with candles, songs, poems, and stories. It was seen as vital that the community be given an opportunity to grieve together. The family most affected by the loss was surrounded by others who had organized and prepared; a kind of mantle of warmth was extended around them.

Several people spoke about the importance of individual connections and dialogue. In one particular tragedy, two children and their mother died in a plane crash. The older boy's teacher decided to visit the father, who was interested in even the smallest stories of what had happened in school during past years. In another school, a teacher visited the parents on a regular basis for more than a year, offering continued care and conversation.

Teachers and parents mentioned the importance of rituals, from planting a tree to creating a special place in the building or school grounds to help everyone remember. "We did not let it go...we held it as a community." Some schools had a corner in the school with photos, flowers, artwork and the child's name. Others had a special poem or song on a regular basis at school gatherings. Once a class did a dramatic performance that dealt with the theme of death and transformation. These efforts had deep meaning for all: "We wanted to keep the family alive to us."

Story content was part of many school experiences, thus the inclusion of them in this book. A story has a way of meeting the needs of diverse listeners, as the imaginative pictures appeal to children and parents at a wide variety of ages.

Advocacy came up in several interview conversations, such as the right of a family to make their own decisions and not just follow the instructions of a funeral home. Questions such as embalming, or bringing the body home, a three-day vigil, and so on are choices that some do not know they can make. I have included a helpful piece from my colleague, Carla Comey in the appendix titled "Bringing Death Home." When we are grieving, it is easy just to follow conventions, but teachers and parents surrounding the family can help open up other possibilities.

The extended family was also mentioned, such as the needs of grandparents who may not be as connected with the values and traditions in a Waldorf school. They, too, need conversation, since each person is on a path of growth, now suddenly accelerated by the experience of a death. It was mentioned that as a society we are continually focused on life and prolonging life, and that we have to learn how to grieve.

Parents spoke with great appreciation for the way teachers modeled the philosophy of Waldorf education and their view of the whole child. A death experience in the community created the possibility for the community to see how spiritual insights can be applied to help and serve. Teachers did not take an anatomical, clinical approach, yet they were clear and embracing of the spiritual origins of each child and the changed relationship that comes through death.

Continuity of care was mentioned, such as regular anniversary celebrations and times to remember and tell stories. One community holds a special gathering each year between November 1st and Advent to bring people together who have suffered a loss. The security and regularity of those gatherings are comforting and healing. The invisible cords that connect people through loss can be made visible at least once a year.

Working with siblings is an area that needed attention. It is harder for sisters and brothers than is often realized. They need to return to a semblance of normality at some point, but when and how?

In summary, all spoke about the importance of involving as many people as possible, and to trust that each person will find their rightful place in the school events. For some it might be providing food, for others an occasional check-in...people have a wonderful way of connecting at a level that is appropriate. And the healing works both ways; those who seem to be walking around just fine are in need as much as those who are overcome. A death is a communion on many levels.

Below are some first-hand accounts, beginning with Anita Brewer-Siljeholm who was a parent at the school now called Waldorf School at Moraine Farm. She shared her reflections in a phone conversation, and then she and Jenny Helmick gave permission to use the article originally published in *Renewal* magazine.

A Son's Passing, A School's Support and Guidance

Anita Brewer-Siljeholm

In October 2004, our son, David, died in an accident while bicycling to the Cape Ann Waldorf School in Beverly Farms, Massachusetts. Quite soon after the event, the school became a guide for me between daily life and the new realm to which our beloved son had gone. I didn't recognize this until recently.

In the days and weeks after that devastating morning, a series of questions arose involving the school and ourselves. Eventually each answer became a choice. Jenny Helmick, David's main lesson teacher, and I have recently reflected on how these choices guided the way one Waldorf school and one family together chose how to respond after a child died one morning on his way to school.

David was fourteen years old when he entered eighth grade in 2004. He was five feet ten inches tall, blond, with a ready smile and a kind, thoughtful, cheerful disposition. His stature in school was that of a "senior diplomat," known to most of the children as a fair-minded and generous boy.

That morning, his ten-year-old sister Marian and I were cycling a short distance behind him on the flat, two-and-a-half-mile route to school. David was ahead of us. While he was passing through the confusing construction zone of a public works project, the rear wheel of his bicycle was knocked aside by a train and he died instantly.

As well as I can understand those moments now, later that day I wanted to complete David's journey by telling to the school in my own words what had happened.

Accompanied by the mother of David's best friend, I left the hospital briefly to visit the school. This was the first, unplanned interaction with the school community after David's passing, and it began a special journey.

I met, standing together in the Main Hall, a group of shocked faculty, staff, and middle school students. We spoke quietly and exchanged what words of comfort we could; I remember explaining that David was not coming back, but that he had not been "squished" by the train, instead that his head was hit so hard that he died. I asked for permission to speak with my daughter's fifth-grade class and did so. The young children solemnly asked a few questions, which I answered, and then I left to return to the hospital where Marian and my husband, John, were with David.

Soon after the news settled in, a question arose about services. Our family planned to begin the services a week after David's death. The school said it would like to have its own ceremony for David, expressing their intent respectfully. I agreed to this, and my family and I attended. It was a solemn, beautiful hour with music played by the faculty, a gospel hymn sung by the middle school students, and words spoken by David's best friend and his teacher. At Jenny's request, as candles were lit, I read a sentence relating to each of David's fourteen years.

A day before the school service, we had a public wake. Shortly after David died, I came to understand that his classmates wanted to see him one more time to say farewell. Wanting to allow them to visit David in privacy, I arranged that the funeral parlor be open to them one hour before it was open to the public. The children and Jenny came early but stayed on for hours, clustered along one wall of the open room near David's body, quietly chatting. The image of their unity and loving courage never left me. Many other visitors lingered at the wake as well.

Around the same time, I asked Jenny if she knew of any guest books more like main lesson books created by students, with their intricate, colorful borders. Traditional guest books felt cramped and sterile. A few days later, to my immense surprise, two large-format, hand-stitched books were handed to me. Every page was differently bordered in color. Some were hand-ruled and others left open, and David's name was inked on each spread. The sturdy paper and clear design offered space for people to write names, essays, poems, short notes—anything at all. The books came to every event, and later on I copied or pasted more messages into them. The attention and care implicit in each colored page have stayed with me, and I continue to refer to them. The books had been made by children in the middle school classes.

As the weeks stretched on into winter, another avenue opened within the Waldorf community. Immediately after the tragedy, a meals delivery system had been set up at school, probably with our permission, though I cannot recall. Every afternoon from mid-October until Christmas, a meal was delivered to our door by a school family. It was an extraordinary gesture, which had unexpected consequences. Since evenings were the time when we found that friends helped most, we often had visitors then. Having the complete meals—usually everything from appetizer to entrees to salads, desserts, and even wine—meant we had food to eat and to share without having to shop and cook, which I was not able to do.

About three weeks after David died, what became known as "the Monday night dinners" started. The basketball season had begun and practice took place after school on Mondays. Remembering how hungry David had been after practice and how long the drive home was for many families, I suggested a meal at our house, which was located closer to the school. This weekly meal became part of our life from that time until graduation in June. Students, coaches, parents, and friends were all welcome without advance notice. Many brought food, but it was never expected. Being together on a regular schedule was extraordinarily helpful for us. Although it was not intended, the delivered meals contributed to our ability to start such a gathering.

The school and our family moved forward together in another way. The class teacher typically chooses the drama that the children put on as their annual class play. That year, though, I was asked for my opinion of the choices: *Antigone* for my daughter's class and *Death Takes a Holiday* for David's. Both scripts directly addressed the subject on all our minds. Trusting the teachers, I agreed.

Marian was willing to play the role of Antigone, a young woman in ancient Greece who begs the king to allow her to retrieve her dead brother's body, and she learned the part with energy. It would have been unimaginable at any other school. In the second play, Death visits mankind over a weekend to learn why he is not beloved. Because a play is for both actors and audience, witnessing the children recite such lines strengthened our ability to live with David's death.

Sometimes the gestures were completely unexpected. The grading quarter ended shortly after David died. To my surprise, an envelope arrived one day from the school containing his progress report, something I had quite forgotten. In full awareness of David's life and his death, his teachers had summoned the grace to write of his final weeks, their hopes and aspirations for him as a student, and their deep sorrow at his passing. Their words remain an extraordinary gift of the highest and deepest order.

Fall and winter passed, and some months later the school and I discussed acknowledging David's presence with a memorial on the wall. I assumed—mistakenly—they meant simply a photo. Just after David died, his teacher brought me the final two watercolors he'd painted. They were among his best. Both works had been painted for a meteorology block in which images of stormy weather and calm weather were assigned. David chose a tropical setting he recalled from a family trip earlier that year. In one image, palm trees slant and bend under a deep grayish-blue sky, whereas in the other painting those same trees stand quietly in the sunshine. High-quality copies of the two paintings were made and incorporated into the memorial display.

In early June, the graduation of David's class was approaching. I was asked if there could be an empty chair with a rose on it to represent David on the stage. I agreed, so while Marian attended with her classmates, I sat with the parents of David's class. The ceremony was beautiful but for me also difficult. I felt the joy implicit in such an event but a terrible sadness, too, as I gazed at David's empty chair and listened to the many moving words that referred to his presence in the class. For the graduation, as for the class plays, the school allowed that a videotape and photos be taken. I am glad now to have them to watch.

Eight years have elapsed since David left. Life has gone on. Classmates are now in college; Marian finished her Waldorf schooling and has graduated from high school; the school now has a permanent campus. To inform the new faculty who did not know David, the school each October reprints the insightful and moving remarks spoken by Jenny Helmick at the memorial service in 2004.

When the school identified the prospective new campus in 2010, our family released and augmented the memorial fund for David to assist with the purchase and renovation costs. During the expansion of the building, a dodecahedron containing four special items was placed within the poured concrete foundation. One item was a sheaf of grasses wrapped in silk representing David. These came from the home he grew up in and his gravesite.

I am not a student of Anthroposophy, but through my years as a Waldorf school parent I have become acquainted with some of Rudolf Steiner's ideas. I know that Steiner holds that when a human being dies, the physical body perishes but the soul and spirit continue to exist. Thus when a loved one passes, the relationship continues. The relationship is unending and important, but of necessity it must change. Although I have many things that represent and remind me of David, I know that David will not reappear. But we can connect and communicate in the spirit instead.

The faculty and staff of the Waldorf school and the whole Waldorf community guided and supported our family after David's passing. They offered countless practical gifts, as well as gestures of soulful, heartwarming consolation. The understanding of death as a transition and a transformation of life, rather than an ending, is perhaps the most valuable gift, one that has sustained me through the inevitable sadness I felt and still feel.

Suanne Campbell, a longtime kindergarten teacher at the Lake Champlain Waldorf School in Vermont, shared some of her reflections first on the phone and then in comments below. She begins with the importance of music.

> I remember three songs that I sang with the children that seemed to be very healing:
>
> 1) Navajo
>   Now I walk in beauty, beauty is before me
>   Beauty is behind me, above and below me

2) Oh great spirit
Earth, wind, sky and sea
you are inside and all around me

This is a song written by Alice Damon (a grandmother to one of the kindergarten children in the class that Joshua was with):

3) Put a circle of white light around you
Put a crown of bright stars on your head
May the fountain of life flow all through
Put two rainbow wings at your back
We are children of the mother
We are children of the father.

We sang these songs often in circle time and also when we walked the labyrinth in front of our school. We always held our hearts and then blew kisses of love to Joshua in the heavens.

The children and I made Joshua a golden silk cape to keep him filled with our love. We dyed the cape golden with marigolds that we had harvested in September. We made him a crown of stars to light his way to heaven. And we made him a sword of light like St. Michael's to help him have courage.

These treasures Joshua wore with him in his casket.

I also picked sunflowers and lovely pink roses that were still blooming in my garden to line the inside of his casket.

It is important to find ways to include children in the death process that are age-appropriate and meaningful.

We also made a banner of dyed silk panels with the children's hands printed in golden paint on them and under it I wrote "We hold you in our hearts with our hands." We gave this banner to Joshua's parents.

There were many times over the year that I made space for the children to share their feelings, to grieve and to smile about our dear friend. Sometimes this happened organically, sometimes more planned by me, most always these sharings took place in nature.

Some children had dreams where Joshua came to them. One child woke up and saw a glorious angel with wings so soft and it was Joshua.

We kept some pictures in the classroom so the children could look at him and remember. This was beautiful to witness.

At the end of the year the parents had a baby doll made that looked like Joshua and the doll's clothes were made of clothes that Joshua wore. They presented this to me while singing our songs. They also gave me a statue of the Madonna.

The love that was shared this year was born out of sadness and connection. We all held each other while we felt held by Joshua.

The preceding stories come from Waldorf communities. The following account by Cindy Long touches on themes and experiences arising from public schools.

Lessons on Loss: How a School Community Heals after a Student Dies

by Cindy Long

Because it was Halloween, sixteen-year-old Melody Ross was dressed up in a Supergirl costume the night she was shot.

She had just left the sold-out Woodrow Wilson High School homecoming football game in Long Beach, California, and was sitting shoulder to shoulder with friends on the school steps, chatting about their team's loss. But before they could make their way inside for the big dance, gunfire erupted, sending hundreds running for cover. Witnesses say between five and seven shots were fired by warring rival gangs.

"Melody Ross was an innocent bystander, caught in the crossfire," says Wilson High head counselor Gayle Marshburn.

The AP honors student and track athlete died at the hospital half an hour later that Friday night. The following Monday, nearly all of Ross's 4,000 fellow students filed into school stunned and saddened. Nobody wanted to stay home, but they couldn't imagine going to class, either. They wanted to talk about what happened. They wanted to hug and cry. They wanted to leave flowers and notes and stuffed bears at a huge memorial erected for Melody at the site of the shooting. But mostly, they wanted to experience the love and support of the school community and mourn the loss of their friend and classmate together.

It's a grim fact of life that every year students from schools across the country will die in accidents, by violence, or from disease.

"It's a sad thing to say, but we usually lose at least one student every year," says Suzanne Huckaba, the head counselor at Central High School in Florence, Alabama, where just this year a junior drowned and a senior was killed in a car accident.

When a student life is lost, the resulting shock and sorrow can shake a school community to its core, but it's that very core that provides the strength to help the other students and staff grieve, and ultimately heal.

"Schools are about young people, and young people are about life. When a young person dies, especially when it's sudden, it completely disrupts the equilibrium of the school environment," says Jerald Newberry, Executive Director of the National Education Association Health Information Network (NEA HIN). "But the care of the school community is what eventually restores balance."

Having a crisis plan in place can help. Published online at http://nea-hin.org/crisisguide/, NEA HIN's School Crisis Guide details the steps a school or district can take before, during, and after a crisis. Having the plan ready before tragedy strikes is essential so that educators know what to do in the days following.

At Woodrow Wilson High School, Mashburn and principal Sandy Blazer put their plan into place immediately. When students returned on the Monday following the shooting, twelve full-time counselors and psychologists were available. Some of them walked the halls; others staffed a crisis center—a designated space stocked with an endless supply of tissues that Marshburn established for students to talk with a counselor and watch a streaming video of Melody created by her classmates.

Mashburn suggests that the most important thing a school can do during the days following a tragic event is to allow community members to express their grief.

Often, those expressions need to be something the students can see and touch. Over the weekend following the shooting, the Wilson High students created a memorial at the spot where Melody was killed. By Monday it towered with balloons, poems, flowers, and other remembrances. Later that day, the entire school and much of the Long Beach community, including the mayor, gathered outside as thirty black balloons were released into the sky.

The students also created a Melody Ross memorial Facebook page, held a candlelight vigil, and, instead of their regular uniforms, wore black T-shirts every day for a week.

But young people aren't the only ones affected by the sudden death of a student.

"We have 157 teachers here and lots of these caring people were struggling after Melody's death," says principal Sandy Blazer. "Some of her actual teachers took it really, really hard. At an emergency faculty meeting, a few teachers broke down."

Some educators were anxious about conducting their classes, so Blazer had counselors fill in for them. Others wanted to be in the classroom, but only to be with the students and talk about losing Melody on homecoming night.

Carol Rea teaches English at Central High School in Alabama. Twice this year she's helped her students come to terms with the loss of a classmate, first when seventeen-year-old Frank Graham, a popular junior, drowned in the Tennessee River, and again when senior Britney Lanier, also seventeen, was killed in a car accident.

Frank was a funny, mischievous student whom everyone called "Bookie." He was swimming with some classmates one Sunday when friends say he cramped up. Unable to make it back to shore, he drowned before they could save him. Most students didn't know until they arrived at school on Monday morning.

Understanding that they were in shock, Rea asked her classes to spend time talking about Frank or writing about him in their journals. "We did this for a couple of days," she says. "Some students wrote pages and pages, others chose not to write at all, but the main thing was to let them express their feelings."

When Britney Lanier was killed in an accident just a few months later, it was a little harder on Rea—Britney was one of her students. They were studying epic heroes of British literature, and Britney had just submitted an essay about a hero in her own life; her grandfather, who had recently been diagnosed with cancer. Rea was deeply moved by Britney's words and gave the essay to her mother, who asked Rea to read it at Britney's funeral a few days later.

"The writing was wonderful, and very personal. It truly revealed Britney as a person," Rea says. "Sharing her essay was a way to celebrate her life and the love she had with her family."

She said class was difficult those first few days following Britney's death. They talked about her smile, and her kindness. They wrote about her in their journals and shared funny stories.

"But it was hard. There was this empty seat in fifth period where she always sat," Rea says. "Nobody wanted to sit there, but we needed to move on. We'll never forget her and she'll be forever etched in our memories. But we need to find closure."

In Long Beach, principal Blazer and counselor Mashburn asked a crisis counselor to talk to the faculty about how to help the school community move on after the shooting. The counselor advised teachers to reconfigure their classrooms so that Melody's chair wouldn't sit empty week after week. He advised against making the desk a shrine because it would serve only as a constant, sad reminder.

He also told them to choose a final date for the memorial at the shooting site. They chose to disassemble the memorial one week later, and they asked Melody's best friends to box up all the remembrances and deliver them to her parents.

Newberry (NEA HIN) agrees that the school should collectively decide on a date to return to routine. But until then, allow students the time for grieving. Kids who are struggling and don't come to classes shouldn't be counted as truant; if they don't turn in their assignments, they should be given an extension. "But after you provide an environment to grieve and mourn for a period of time, it's important to return to normalcy as soon as possible," says Newberry. "Returning to a regular routine is essential to healing."

Two weeks after Melody's murder, Wilson High hosted its next home game. Melody's parents and family were there, along with the mayor and chief of police. The football players normally wear "W" stickers on their helmets, but they turned them upside down to "M," for Melody. The game began with a moment of silence, and it ended with a Wilson win of 47 to 3, which they dedicated to Melody.

It was the team's way of saying goodbye.

"I've never been so proud of Wilson High School," says principal Blazer. "I've been there thirty-eight years, and have never seen so much love among our students. We're stronger as a result."*

---

* NEA Student Death: The Empty Desk (http://www.na.org/home/38144.htm).

6

Spiritual Perspectives on Death

*Ram Dass said, "What if we could view death as just another stage of life?"**

How do we view death? Do we take our mental images from the movies? If so, it is interesting to at least compare the images that reveal attitudes in the likes of *Indiana Jones*, *Star Wars*, or *Ender's Game*. There is often more spirituality portrayed in the entertainment business than one might at first imagine. In many cases, there are suggestions that there is more to death than simply the cessation of life. Indeed, in some popular films Ram Dass was able to observe affirmations of death as another stage.

Others today carry a fear of death. For those who have either a physical or mental illness, death can be a constant menace, a reality that must be wrestled with on a daily basis. Even with seemingly healthy young people I meet, the question of death often arises. For some, there have been near-death experiences or attempts at suicide. Death is often an unseen but potent companion on the journey.

In 1917, during the final months of carnage brought on by World War I, Rudolf Steiner affirmed that for so many, death is always present in some fragmentary way in our mental images, and that when it actually happens it is a summation of all the "breakdown activities constantly at work in us. Of course much of this breakdown is counteracted, although in the end it does result in spontaneous death. We must understand death

---

* See https://www.ramdass.org/view-death-just-another-stage-life.

as an active force in the organism just as we understand life forces." (Selg, p. 105)

So death is an ongoing process, a permanent feature of human existence and our past-oriented sensory–nervous system. As described in *Foundations of Human Experience* and many other places, we know that the nervous system is continually dying, thus making conceptual thinking possible. We are able to provide the physical basis for conceptual activity through the dying process of the nerves. The actual moment of physical death at the end of our human life on Earth is an intensification of a process that is actually ongoing through life. But in that we attain our freedom, and so much of what we consider human achievement, through thinking, we can see this ongoing aspect as a kind of birthing. Each idea is a new birth. And we see how the soul–spiritual activity (thinking) and the bodily–material processes (nerves) work together on an intimate basis.

Through our intellect we can comprehend and exercise freedom, but in order to do so we need the nerves, the dying element within us. Through our actions, our will, we are able to comprehend in a different way and connect to what is living. When we are able to channel our will into our thinking we can achieve sense-free thinking that makes us independent beings. We are able to transcend the organic life–death process when we think (Steiner, 1996, p. 68).

At the end of life, our physical body is either cremated or buried. Most consider that the end of the line, and it is in many respects. However, in lecture 3 of *The Foundations of Human Experience,* Rudolf Steiner introduces an environmental aspect. Just as yeast activates the dough in baking bread, so the corpse adds an active ingredient to the earth when it is placed in the soil:

> The forces that earthly development continually receives through the acceptance of human corpses, that is, the forces contained in these corpses supports the evolution of the Earth. Without the support of such forces today, minerals could no longer unfold the forces of crystallization...through such forces, plants that no longer could grow are able to grow today. (ibid., p. 71)

He goes on to say that animals and humans are also assisted in their skeletal structure and nerve–sense development. Why? The material that is found in the corpse is "transformed matter," not the same material that was there at birth. Through life on Earth the material substance of the body changes, is renewed. One could say that matter is infused with spirit, the higher intentions that we bring with us through our living and acting while alive. The Earth needs us, and it needs a death process in order to remain alive!

This is one of the reasons why those who have become social activists concerning funeral home practices are so spot-on. Families need more choices in how a body is handled, and around the time frame used from death to burial or cremation. Marianne Dietzel and others have made real progress in funeral home advocacy. The three-day wake, for instance, is a necessary stage in the process, both for those who are grieving, but also for the departed. Embalming has consequences, as does the use of other chemical agents. This is not the place to go into detail, but as with other social justice issues, we need advocates for family choice.

Many in our Western culture today are *thanatophobic,* or fear death. This can be seen in how we turn over so many decisions to others in the funeral process, or even the language used in obituaries. Death is often described in the local paper as having come "after a long battle" that someone "fought courageously," or as "the loss of our dear friend." These phrases are understandable, yet the message is often one that says death is a defeat. Likewise, many in our culture today are taught to deny death, avoid discussion of it, and do everything to appear healthy even when struggling. The cosmetic industry thrives on anti-aging techniques, and advertisements herald the latest creams and products that ward off the advance of natural aging.

We need to transform our attitudes and practices around death, just as we have had to do with educational and environmental issues. We need to lift our gaze from the purely physical aspects of death to find new spiritual perspectives that can release our fear and aversion to death. For many, death is a release, not just a tragedy.

One of my recent Antioch students, Teresa Corbo, wrote a paper in which she reintroduced me to the work of Thích Nhất Hạnh and his book *No Death, No Fear*. He describes the Buddhist view that there is really no birth or death, just manifesting of different conditions of existence. When conditions are no longer good for a person's life, death occurs (Thích, p. 5). We never go into nothingness. Using examples from nature, Thích Nhất Hạnh compares people as waves, some large and some smaller. A wave might be fearful that it might die, but it doesn't realize that it is always part of the larger ocean. It is never-ending (ibid., p. 23). We should not grieve for something that is beautiful and always manifesting. Nothing is the same from one moment to the next; impermanence means that everything is constantly changing. Just as flowers come and go in a garden, so do all things in life.

My research assistant, Katlyn Boucher, had the following reflections after typing some of the material for this chapter:

> What if every child and adult knew of this wisdom—that the spirit continues on after death. Approaching the human experience "chapter" as the ultimate learning ground as a spiritual being—for sensing, feeling, and manifesting that is uniquely human. Where most enter Earth and become trained to forget our eternal beingness and come to a crux where they can continue to forget or spend much of their adult lives remembering and blooming further into the spiritual being having a human experience.
>
> What if all of this wisdom was followed by knowing that in fact, death means going on into a more beautiful portion of their development as a spiritual being.
>
> How come death is not approached as a congratulations for "graduating" from the human experience chapter of the spiritual being's eternity? Is the cause of grief a shattering of one's expectations? An assumption on some level that this person, or animal, would be around longer than the contracts they set up with God, to be here? Is grief the process of coming to terms with one's own underlying expectations? What would grief look like if expectations weren't there? Would grief be any different?
>
> Did the correlation for speaking and researching grief correlate with our disconnect with the spiritual realm and working with our dead loved ones? When did death become a great tragedy/separation

vs. a metamorphosis? When did we become a culture that discarded our loved ones who have passed, in our souls vs. holding them in love?

This brings us back to Ram Dass and the view that death is just another stage in life.

What happens right after death? According to Steiner, in the first few days we see a tableau that omits all subjective experiences from our earthly journey. While we are alive we always have feelings of pain or pleasure, joy or sadness, and so on. What we perceive is always linked to inner activity, especially in the realm of feeling. However, during the tableau immediately after death, our joys and sorrows are no longer attached to these feeling images of life. We see the tableau as objectively as if we were looking at a painting in a museum. In a remarkably short period of time all the pictures of our life are spread out before us (Selg, p. 115).

Then gradually the astral body begins to dissolve and the soul habits of earthly life are released. This breaking of old habits occurs in the sphere of warmth. We are called upon to renounce old habits, feelings and aspirations. Most interesting of all, from my point of view, we now experience the consequences of our own actions from the perspective of those who have been affected by them. As we work back through a past life, we get to see the other half of our deeds, the part others experienced. Thus this recapitulation involves a moral assessment of one's own biography.

From this comes what Steiner calls "karmic will," an urge to work in new ways in the next life. At the midnight hour of the soul, the individual resolves to reincarnate in a new body, with new parents, in a new location on Earth in such a way as there are possibilities for applying the lessons learned from the journey after death.

7

The Legend of Baldur

Some years ago my family visited a butterfly museum in south Florida. We were treated to a spectacular array of colors as we strolled through the various enclosures, watching the exotic birds, butterflies and unusual plants. At one point Ionas (then age eleven) stopped in front of a simple case on the wall and simply stood there quietly. Karine and I noticed his curiosity and joined him. He was looking at a few rows of white/gray objects clinging to the inside surface. For the most part they looked quite dry and nondescript. But with excitement he pointed to one near the top right-hand corner and said, "Look, it is growing." At first there was little to confirm his observation. But we stayed and watched.

After a few moments we all saw that the object was indeed growing, swelling, more on one side than the other. Then, as Ionas sucked in his breath in astonishment, we watched as the cocoon began to open, some color emerged, and then within seconds, a most beautiful purple butterfly emerged. It opened its wings completely and remained hovering in suspended animation. We looked at each other and knew that we had witnessed a miracle.

What had appeared so dead was now alive. We had participated in the mystery of death and the miracle of life.

When I returned home after that vacation, while searching for footnote material for a book I was completing on Initiative, I stumbled upon a folder of notes I had been collecting for many years. It was a collection of lectures and materials on the theme of the Norse God, Baldur. Glancing through the folder, the questions just started to spring out at me: What is the meaning of Baldur's death? Why is death so prominent in many of our lives today? How can we understand the sacrifice of a child's life? How can the story of Baldur, the most beloved of the Norse Gods, help us understand the loss of youth in today's world?

So here is the story of Baldur.*

The Death of Baldur

Never without sorrow was the life of the gods. Always some trouble threatened them. Every day and every hour they had to ward off some enemy. But as long as Baldur the Bright dwelled among them, the powers of evil could not fully come to the fore. Baldur watched over the dreams of man. Night after night he showed man the greatness and scope of the working of the gods. Therefore his castle was called Breidablick, for from it the soul could look far and wide into the world of the gods. And as long as these dreams were not darkened the life of the gods could make itself known to the senses of man.

But this was to change. Dreamless and ever darker did man's sleep become. It was this darkening that, in the Edda, are called "Baldur's dreams telling of woe." For his dreams cannot be thought of apart from those of human beings.

Terror gripped the gods when they learned of this. At Urd's Well they met, under the hallowed ash—gods and goddesses. It was not hard for them to read the meaning of the darkness that had come over the once-bright dream of Baldur. Death-bearing was this darkness.

Then Odin resolved to ride to Niflheim, for there he knew the grave of the oldest of all seers, Sikyls. He saddled Sleipnir, his steed, and rode past the gate of Hel, where the hound Garm barked long at him. Eastward he rode to the grave. There he got down and began to sing mightily and rousing songs of magic. Long he had to sing. Only slowly the long-dead awakened, rose with great trouble, and spoke:

> Who are you, man,
> Not known to me,
> Who called me to tread
> The toilsome path?

---

* Dan Lindholm, *Götter-Schicksal Menschen-Werden* (God's destiny becoming human).

> With snow I was covered,
> Beaten with rain,
> Bedecked with dew.
> Long dead was I.

Odin answered and called himself *Wegtam*. "One accustomed to the road." Then he began to ask, "For Whom are Hel's benches adorned with shining gold, for whom the seat strewn with rings?"

The Wala spoke, "Here the hall is trimmed for Baldur. The tankard with foaming mead stands ready. A shield lies across it. The Asa's kin at Hel's are full of expectation. I spoke because I was made to. Now I will be silent."

Yet Odin went on with his asking. "Do not be silent, Wala. You shall speak until I know all. Tell me, who will bring death to Baldur? Who must bear the guilt when he must go from the gods?"

"Hodur shall show the Highborn Son to Helheim, he will be the cause of the grief. I spoke because I was made to. Now I will be silent.

Yet Odin asked further. He wanted to know who should avenge Baldur, and lastly this: "Who of the women will not want to weep? Who will with joy throw her kerchief toward heaven?"

Who this woman would be, would be known all too soon. But from this question the Wala knew who stood before her. "You are not Wegtam, but Odin, the ancient god," she said—and with that forced herself from his spell.

"And you are not the Wala, not the prophetess, but the mother of the Norns!" Odin called after her as she vanished.

When Odin came back to Asgard, Frigga, Baldur's mother, had gone forth into the wood to ask of every being and every thing an oath that they would do no harm to her son. A far journey—yet every being and every thing swore the oath: fire and water, iron and ore, stone and earth, herb and tree, animals, birds, poison and pestilence.

The gods rejoiced, and to honor Baldur they held a feast. There he stood amidst his brothers. They honored him by shooting arrows at him, throwing stones, or wielding their swords against him. Like a miracle it seemed to them, for nothing could harm Baldur.

Only one was watching the game full of envy. That was Loki. The happiness of the gods was always a thorn in his flesh. He took the shape of an old woman and went to Frigga.

"How happy," began the wicked hag, "the game of the Asa sounds from Idafield. And nothing can harm Baldur?" "Nothing on Earth will harm him," said Frigga, "for no one denied me the oath."

"But are you sure that everyone and everything were asked?"

Then Frigga confessed that to the west of Walhalla she had met a plant that had seemed to her too young to swear such a weighty oath: the mistletoe.

Now the hag knew what she wanted to know. And Loki did not tarry in looking for the mistletoe in order to cut an arrow from it. With this arrow he crept to the playing field of the gods. Hodur stood there, a little apart from the joyful throng. To him, blind brother of Baldur, Loki went. "Why do not you, like the others, honor your brother?" "Because I cannot see him," answered Hodur.

Then Loki offered to aim for him, so that Hodur also might honor Baldur.

"Here, take the arrow and put it to the string," he said. "My eye shall serve you."

And Hodur took the arrow from Loki's hand and shot it.

Thus happened that greatest misfortune that ever befell. For the arrow pierced Baldur. The bright god fell dead to the ground.

When Baldur had fallen none of the Asas could speak. Instead of attending to the corpse they let their arms hang idle. They looked at the unhappy murderer. But they could take no revenge, for the ground on which they stood was peace-hallowed. And when they tried to speak they broke into loud wailing.

But none was touched as closely by the deed as Odin. He foresaw, as no other could, what this loss must bring to gods and men.

At last, when the Asas had collected themselves a little, Frigga spoke. "I shall ask," she said, "which of my sons is minded to gain all my love and favor? Who is so minded, let him ride down to Hel and offer ransom for Baldur."

The brave Hermod offered himself, and Odin lent him Sleipnir. Hermod mounted the steed of the god and started on his way.

The Asas carried the corpse of the god to the sea. There, propped on the beach, stood his large and valiant ship, Ringhorn. On this ship they erected a bier for the corpse. Much wood was piled up, for the gods wanted to prepare for Baldur a fire voyage. But when everything was ready and the ship was to be pushed into the water the gods' strength failed them. They had to send to Jotunheim for an old hag called Hyrrokin. Hyrrokin came riding on a wild wolf whom she bridled with adders. The monster was so fierce that four Berserkers had to hold it while Hyrrokin pushed the boat into the sea. This she did with such force that fire and sparks flew from the rollers.

When Nana, the wife of the dead god, saw this her heart burst with sorrow. So she wailed on the bier beside Baldur, and then the boat was decked with gold and jewels and set aflame. Odin sacrificed his ring Draupnir, Thor hallowed the flames with Mjollnir, his hammer.

Of Hermod's journey to Hel it is told that he rode for nine nights through deep valleys and dark gorges. He saw nothing until he came to the banks of the river Gjak. This river is spanned by a bridge that is covered with gold all over. There, by the bridge, sits a guard. When she saw Hermod she asked him his name and his country. "Your cheeks do not have the color of one who has died. Five armies of dead rode across last night. The bridge thunders more loudly with you alone than with all of them." Then she showed Hermod his further way. "If you would find Hel's house, ride northward and downward."

A high fence went around Helheim. The gate was heavily barred. Hermod dismounted his horse and tightened the girth. Then he jumped into the saddle again and spurred Sleipnir so that he leapt high above the gate.

When he entered the hall Hermod saw his brother Baldur enthroned on the high seat. His face was pale and full of sorrow. One night Hermod stayed in the house of Hel. Then he offered the gods' ransom for Baldur. He also told of how deep was the mourning for Baldur. Hel answered that she would see proof of the great love professed for Baldur. "If all things in the world, living and dead, will weep for Baldur, then he may

The Legend of Baldur

return to Asgard. But if the eyes of anyone remain dry Baldur shall stay in Helheim henceforth." With this counsel Hermod had to leave the hall. Baldur went with him to the threshold and gave him the ring Draupnir that he might take it back to Odin.

When he came to Asgard, Hermod told the gods what he had learned on his journey to Hel. Then the Asas sent messengers forth into the world to beg that every thing and every being might help with their tears to ransom Baldur from Hel.

And all wept their tears; men, animals, trees, grass, stones, and ore; the dew makes drops, rosin oozes, stones become moist when they are taken from the cold to a warm place. When the messengers were on their way home with the good tidings that everything had wept tears for Baldur they saw an old woman in a cave. She called herself *Thok*.

Now Thok answered:

> Dry are the tears
> That Thok weeps
> By Baldur's bier.
> Living or dead—
> He never liked me.
> Let Hel keep
> What now she has.

There she sat, the old hag, after whom Odin asked when the Wala would answer no more.

Who was she?

If not Loki himself, then one by Loki ruled.

The death of Baldur was the result of a threefold exception:

1. The one substance that did not take "the pledge" was the mistletoe, which was deemed too insignificant to cause any trouble.
2. The dart was cast by the one player who could not "play," namely the blind Hodur who had stood on the sidelines as the others made sport of Baldur's seeming invincibility. Most of us have experienced what it is like to be on the "outside," to be different, to be disconnected. This feeling must only have been accentuated by the fact that the person in question was blind, thus emphasizing his lack of participation.

3. The guidance and direction for the dart was provided by Loki in disguise, yet another layer of exceptionality. A disguise means you are not what you appear to be.

Thus, at the very outset one has to regard the moment of Baldur's death as ruled by an unusual set of exceptional factors. What is cast under so many veils of exceptionality has the unusual potential to overthrow the old order, to disrupt the normal course of events.

Most of us have developed a close relationship to the ordinary, the day-in day-out flow of routine that can at times lull us to a state of waking sleep. For every conscious act we perform, such as writing an email, there are countless accompanying acts that occur beneath the radar of consciousness. These actions are often deeply seated in our habit life—running a hand through one's hair, wiggling toes while sitting, reverting to old thought patterns, responding instinctively to someone else, pretending to listen while attending elsewhere, and so on. These things happen continuously all day long, and they are often deep-seated. If they were allowed to rule us completely, we would become more and more like a creature living an instinctual life and less and less human. Although we might feel somewhat safe and comfortable in our habit life, if left alone it could become a kind of death trap for the creative, wakeful human spirit.

Often life hands out an exceptional situation or event that serves as a summons, a call to rouse ourselves from the semi-sleep of the habit life. These exceptional situations take on a variety of forms: a change of job, birth of a child, a move to a new apartment or house, a divorce, or the death of a friend or loved one. Suddenly we are roused, conscious of things we had not realized before, and resolve to take up life in a new way. The human spirit shakes off, so to speak, the heavy mantle of the habit life and we have an opportunity to make a fresh start.

Of course, sometimes these opportunities are transitory and the moment is lost and we gradually sink back into the old stupor. But in most cases, I have found that these exceptional events are formative and life-changing. Indeed, one of the most sacred of all human attributes is the ability to change and learn from life. The "dart" that pierces and even draws some blood is often the one that wakes us and stimulates a higher level of consciousness.

The dart that killed Baldur was fashioned out of mistletoe, which is used today in anthroposophical clinics to prepare iscador, a treatment for cancer, the illness of our time. For insight into the remarkable mistletoe plant, see the appendix.

The Meaning of Lamentation

In olden times, many people around the world had an intimate connection to nature. Every tree, bush, and animal spoke to those who would listen. Legends and myths that far back in time are full of the many and varied connections between nature and mankind. Rather than just a sentimental feeling, one could say that in their hearts, their souls, they had a holy feeling of comfort. Through nature they were able to experience the divine. The forces of nature were rejuvenating; they helped shape and form the vibrancy experienced in all living things. On many levels, humans lived in a happy union with nature.

Then a significant transition took place. Rudolf Steiner used an example to illustrate this change: Imagine a situation in which we see all the colors in the world around us, the flowers, the blue-greens of the forests, the sunlight dancing on lakes, the blue sky. Then imagine a kind of revolution in human perception in which gradually the colors fade and eventually the whole of nature appears only gray upon gray, so when one looked down at the flowers one saw only shades of gray. The same could be described when one looked up to the sky or out into the forests. This is just an example that illustrates the mighty change in human perception in regard to nature. Previously human beings could see spirit in nature, forces working and speaking through nature. Now that all became frighteningly silent. The old way of seeing gradually vanished and died away.

And when people asked what had happened that nature was now deprived of its godly element, the spiritual leaders of the Norse people would answer, "There was once in the world of gods, Baldur, who united in himself the force of the sunlight. But Baldur, on account of his hatred of the dark elements, had to transfer his dwelling place that he had extended to the horizon of men's Earth, to Hel in the underworld. The force of vision of the old times vanished. The clear sunlight was submerged, the shining radiance of the old gods was lost, and only the dead semblance of the sunlight was reflected through the light of the Moon's sickle. The world has become material. Nature over which men lament, over which they mourn, which they charge with the concepts of sin and guilt, this nature appears like the mourning survivor that was once united with the divine and that sent into all souls the ray of the divine. And thus arose the feeling that the people had when they heard the death song of the old Sun god Baldur" (Steiner, 1981, p. 97).

This sense of loss caused great lamentation, great sorrow for all who remained on the Earth. It was now apparent that Baldur was no longer an active Sun presence on the Earth, but from now on would work from the other side, the world of the invisible. There was also a sense that from the underworld, the power of Baldur would be insufficient, that something else would be needed to bring the forces of renewal back to the Earth.

In many European countries the bells fall silent on Good Friday. For many Christians, the world becomes mute and utterly silent to mark the descent of Christ into the depths of the Earth following the path of Baldur. The world is asked to wait, to hold the silence.

Odin and the gods of old were not able to bring Baldur back, as not all things agreed to weep for him. But with the Mystery of Golgotha, the silent waiting had a different outcome. Because of the soul preparation through intimate experience of Baldur's death, the experience of Christ's death and sacrifice were ever so much more living. Just as in the past the Aesir would look down upon the Earth and witness Baldur in his power giving life to nature, now humanity could experience new life through the unity of Christ with the Earth.

The path through death is experienced every year by those who follow the sequence of Good Friday, Holy Saturday, and the Resurrection on Sunday. It was felt that all the earthly experiences death, as with Baldur, and that in death was the germ, the possibility of new life. Through the death of Baldur many were able to participate in a process of a special kind, an experience that was a precursor to a new stage in human evolution: "For the sake of the further development of humankind, death must intervene in earthly evolution in an increasingly intense way" (Steiner, 1981, p. 101). Through a process of differentiated feeling, human beings can emerge to see the life-giving Sun force of Baldur in the elemental world after it has experienced death. Each year, we see in nature the life-death-life process before our very eyes.

Then came the event of Golgotha and the event in which Christ united Himself with death. Through this, human beings were given the possibility of new life, for "Christ has the power, when we take Him up into our soul forces, again to awaken what was lost through Baldur's death. As Baldur appeared through the winds and the waves, so the Christ also appeared in the winds and the waves" (ibid., 102). A force that works through nature, through wind and waves, has now become the power of Christ who can also still the wind and waves, but now nature has become divine. Like the disciples in the wooden ship that comes safely to land, the people of the Earth can now say "God be praised," for the child of God has delivered the people out of their distress. The lamentation is over.

Tears

> Thok she weepeth
> With dry tears
> For Baldur's death—
> Neither in life, nor yet in death,
> Gave he me gladness.
> Let Hel keep her prey.*

Crouching in her cave, Thok was unmoved and refused to weep for the death of Baldur, thus ending any hope that he might be released and return to the lands of the living. What does this mean, a refusal to weep? What is the significance of crying, shedding tears?

When Faust was on the verge of killing himself, he suddenly heard the ringing of the Easter bells, whereupon he cried out, "The tear wells up, to

---

* "Elder Edda," Guerber, *Myths of the Norsemen*, p. 212.

earth I am restored" (Goethe, p. 22). The great poet, scientist and author Goethe thus uses tears as a way to indicate Faust's return to the world.

Let us say we lose a close friend or loved one. With this loss, part of our soul is torn away. A bond on the physical plane between the two of us is broken, and there is a great feeling of sorrow. We suffer at this breaking of the bond, and there is an inner feeling that a part of us has departed as well. Something is torn from our very being, our inmost self, and this shattered sense presses itself on our consciousness, or what Steiner calls the astral body. This compression of consciousness works right into the physical body and is expressed as tears. One could say that tears are an outer expression of a grief-stricken soul contracting.

The tears are not merely an outflow, they are a kind of compensation for the stricken sense of self, or ego. What was formerly enriched by stimuli from the outer world is now deprived and finds inner recompense through tears. "If an ego that has suffered a loss lets go as far as shedding tears, these tears, in raising the ego's consciousness to awareness of its loss, give it a certain subconscious feeling of wellbeing.... But it does restore balance" (Steiner, 2006, p. 32). When crying, the breathing also changes: in-breathing becomes shorter and shorter, and the out-breathing longer and longer. The opposite is true of laughing, in which the soul expands and the in-breathing becomes longer.

If the connection of crying and laughing to breathing and the ego is still not clear, one has only to remember the creation story in the Old Testament. Yahweh, or Jehovah, breathed the breath of life into the first human being, thus endowing him with a living soul.

> Tragedy presents us with a spectacle that does indeed contract the astral body and so impart firmness and inner cohesion to the ego. Comedy , on the other and, expands the astral body inasmuch as people raise themselves above follies and coincidences, and it thereby encourages liberation of the ego....
>
> In human nature there is a kind of pendulum that has to swing to and fro between what leads, on the one hand, to tears and, on the other, to laughter. The ego can progress only by being in movement. If the pendulum were at rest, the ego would not be able to increase or develop and would succumb to inner death....

> If we ask what a laugh expressed by the human face actually is, we now know that it is the spirit telling us that here we see human beings endeavoring to find liberation from being entangled in things unworthy of them, and raising themselves with a smile above the things they may never allow to enslave them. And tears in our eyes are telling us of the spiritual fact that—even when people feel that the thread linking them to another living creature is broken—they are still trying to find the bridge. And when they strengthen their ego through tears, they are emphatically saying, "I belong to the world, and the world belongs to me, for I cannot bear being torn away from it. (ibid., pp. 41–43)

The story of Baldur is the heart-wrenching story of being torn away from the old world and being totally uncertain of what is to follow. It speaks to some of the deepest aspects of the human condition: our vulnerability to death, betrayal and suffering. Despite all our material comforts, there are things in life we cannot avoid. Just as Odin rode down into the underworld to confront Hel, so we need the courage to face death. Tears can help us find ourselves again, as described above, but in the end we each have to walk our own path. No one can do it for us. The path of the modern human being is that of the consciousness soul. It is one fraught with struggle, but in the end, we can achieve a state of freedom that comes from within (not directed by the "gods" or another authority). We have lost our innocence as a society, but have gained new possibilities for choice and the exercise of human freedom. Can we become worthy of this new opportunity? Those who, like Baldur, have crossed the threshold, are ever so eagerly waiting for our response.

8

The Golden Casket

Herbert Hahn*

In a large golden house there lived a father with many children. One day he said to one of his sons, "Now it is time for you to begin your journey." He led him to a staircase that seemed bottomless, with many steps winding around and down. He accompanied his son a few steps and then spoke to him: "Now I must leave you. But I shall give you one thing that you must take care of," and he gave his son a golden casket, which the boy immediately folded into his garment. "Always carry this with you," said the father. "It will guard and protect you. But do not open it until you come back to me."

With these words the father said goodbye, and the son began to climb down the many steps. As he was arriving at the bottom he turned to look back up the way he had come, but was amazed to see that the staircase had disappeared, and in its place rose a steep black wall. And before him stretched a flat white surface that undulated up and down; it was the ocean.

As he could go neither backward nor forward, the son began to feel heartsick. Then he saw, way out on the water, something moving toward him. It was a boat with no rudder, steering wheel or mast. Lightly it came to rest on the shore, inviting him to climb aboard. Since he had no alternative he jumped in, and the boat immediately took off, carrying him swiftly out onto the ocean. Soon he could no longer see the black wall.

At first the journey was peaceful; soon, however, a brisk wind arose and blew stronger and stronger. The waves now had whitecaps, and the

---

* Translation from German by Torin Finser.

boat began to heave to and fro. The wind soon became a mighty gale, tossing the little boat back and forth like a nutshell. The son could hear and see nothing besides the howling gale and black sky; he was barely able to cling to the side of the boat. All of a sudden there was a great jolt as the boat struck a sharp rock, tearing a hole in the bottom. Water streamed in, and the boat began to sink.

The son was sure he would drown if he stayed in the boat and decided it would be better to be in the water. So he jumped into the turbulent waves, grasping the golden casket with his left hand, close to his heart. No sooner had he jumped in, however, a wonderful thing happened; the storm suddenly abated. The water became smooth, and as he began to swim a strong current pushed him slightly to his left. It was as if the golden casket were leading him onward.

It is hard to say how long he swam, but at last he saw land ahead. As he stepped onto the shore of the large island, he was startled by a crowd of excited people shouting, "A king! A new king!" Before he knew it, a crown had been placed upon his head and a beautiful mantle around his shoulders. The people lifted him up and carried him inland, cheering and shouting with joy. More and more people joined them, and soon a great procession had formed. Flutes, trumpets and drums accompanied the crowds.

As the procession came to the castle, it entered a banquet hall filled with an array of delicious food and drink offered by cooks and servants. As the crowd ate, drank, laughed and talked, no one noticed the new arrival sitting there with shock and confusion on his face. As the music and noise of the party grew so loud that not a word could be understood, the son hardly felt able to breathe after his long journey. He wondered what was happening, and what would happen next.

Looking around the crowded room, he spotted an old man sitting quietly. He must have been very old; his hair and beard were white. He seemed kindly, though his expression was serious and his smile was sad. Nobody noticed as the son arose and gestured to the old man that he wanted to speak. They went to a nearby room. "Will you please tell me what all this means?" asked the son.

"I will, my king," answered the old man. "But am I really a king?" the son asked incredulously. "You are a king, but only for a short time." Then the old man told him that every year, a stranger arrived on the shores of the island and was greeted with great pomp and circumstance. While he was king, he could enjoy anything he wanted; his every wish, no matter how small, would be granted upon his royal command.

"However, when a year has passed," said the old man, "all the festivities come to an end." He told the son that exactly twelve months after his arrival, the very same people who had greeted the new king would pull him off the throne, rip the crown off his head and tear off the royal mantle. Once again as poor as he came, the deposed king would be led back to the beach and made to board a boat in which he could neither sit nor stand, but only lie down. The boat would carry him out over the ocean to a silent and empty wasteland where everything is desolate and gray.

In that land there are no trees, not a blade of grass, not a worm moving in the soil, not a moth in the air, not a bird to sing. "Yes, that is how it ends," said the old man, with downcast eyes. "But that is terrible!" cried the young king. "With all this celebration, this feasting, this awful music. Tell me, is there no other way to avoid the journey to the wasteland? "

"I have told you all that I'm allowed to say," said the old man. "The rest you must find out for yourself. But it is a good sign that you are already asking me on the first day; none of the other kings have done that." As the old man spoke, the son saw a faint glimmer in his eye.

The young king thanked his wise adviser with all his heart. He thought to himself, "If I am the king, I must start acting like one." He returned to the festival hall and announced that the party was over. He told the cooks, servants and boisterous musicians to go home. Then the young king went to his bedroom and contemplated all the strange things that had happened. He decided to face the future with courage, and before he went to sleep he placed under his pillow the golden casket he had so faithfully protected.

That night he had a strange dream. He heard a voice that seemed vaguely familiar saying, "Go to the poor, the sick, and the lonely."

The Golden Casket

The king awoke shortly before dawn with those words ringing in his ears; they were as if engraved on his heart. And so it was that this morning he turned away all the people who came to him with offers of service, and ignored the golden carriage with white horses that awaited his pleasure. Instead he asked for a simple cart, a doctor and a single servant, and began to follow the counsel of his dream. He visited the hovels of the poor; he stood at the bedside of the sick; he climbed down into the darkest dungeons to see prisoners long forgotten by humanity. How great was the suffering on all sides! Spurred on by the words from his dream, which he carried in his heart, he had days, weeks, months of work to do. There was no time to rest.

The people in the castle were dissatisfied and said they hardly noticed that they had a king any more. But it was quite different elsewhere on the island; many faces now looked as radiant as if they had seen sunlight for the first time in their lives.

Half a year passed in this way. When the king passed his old adviser from time to time, they exchanged friendly looks, and the king was encouraged and believed he was on the right path. But then one day, the old man wore his sorrowful expression again. So the king stopped to ask, "Have I not done the right thing?" "I believe that indeed you have done much good," answered the old man, "but perhaps not all has happened that should have come to pass." He stopped then, and the king noticed he wanted to say more but could not.

Yet what must still come to pass? Had he overlooked or neglected anything? The king thought and thought, deep into the night. Suddenly he remembered that it had been many nights since he had put the golden casket under his pillow. He did so, and his worries seemed to lift. When he fell asleep, the familiar voice spoke again: "Build ships, build many ships. Fill them with all that grows, all that blooms, all that bears fruit. Send the ships out onto the sea wherever the wind will take them. But no person must be aboard."

When the king awoke, he carefully collected the words he had heard and placed them in his heart. On that very day he called all the carpenters and craftsmen together, everyone who could help build ships. And now they began a great bustle of hammering and sawing, and all who watched were astonished as one ship after another was built and sent out to sea. The ships carried no people but were filled with young fruit trees, shrubs, anything that could flower and bear fruit. Every time a ship set sail, the king stood on the shore and watched as it gradually disappeared from sight. Meanwhile he continued to care for the sick, the poor and the lonely. By now, very few prisoners remained on the island.

Now the day arrived on which the year was over. The king remembered everything the old man had told him, and prepared himself for what must happen. He knelt to say his morning prayers, holding the golden casket close to his heart. Now he heard voices outside his room, growing louder and louder until they sounded like a storm brewing. Then suddenly it was quiet. "Now they will come in," thought the king, "and tear everything off me that belongs to the king. May it come to pass."

But when the door opened, only one man entered. He had languished a long time in a dark prison but was now free. He said, "The hour is come and the highest law of the island is all-powerful; we must now bid you farewell. But what we have done to earlier kings we will not do to you. There is no hand that wishes to rip the crown and the king's mantle from you. Take them off yourself, and then I will accompany you on your way."

Without hesitation the king did what was required and took off his crown and mantle. Then, clad only in the thin garment in which he had arrived, he walked out of the castle. As he made his way out onto the street, he saw to the right and left a thick wall of people standing in the deepest silence, signifying their immense thanks and pure love.

As the son came to down to the shore, he saw the ocean sparkling before him. There was no breath of wind, yet in the distance he saw a boat approaching as if driven by an unseen power. When it landed before him, he remembered the great law of the island and obediently lay down in the boat. Immediately he fell asleep and was surrounded by a wonderful deep dream.

He did not know how long the journey took; he awoke when the boat hit something with a jolt. This must be the shore of the lonely, desolate

The Golden Casket

wasteland. Slowly he roused himself, climbed out of the boat and took a few steps. But as he looked around, he was surprised; no desolation met his gaze. Instead, soft grass was underfoot, trees bloomed with the promise of fruit, and birdsong could be heard everywhere. The son rubbed his eyes. This could not be the desolate gray land that the old man had spoken of! Perhaps he was still dreaming?

Then he remembered all the ships he had sent forth; they must have landed in this desolate place, and invisible hands must have planted the grass and trees, transforming the island. Then in front of him, the son saw once again the tall, steep black wall. He realized that he had crossed the great ocean. His heart beat quickly and he moved toward the wall as if propelled by an invisible hand. As he began to climb the winding staircase that unfolded before him, he heard far above the voice of his father calling to him. With unimaginable joy he climbed further and further up.

The father reached his arms out to him and asked, "Have you brought the golden casket home with you?" "Yes father, I have." "Have you opened it?" "No," answered the son, "I left it closed as you instructed." "It is well that you followed my command. Now you may open it."

The son did as his father asked and opened the casket. Inside it he discovered his father's house, with its golden pillars and his many brothers and sisters going in and out or seated at the great table. Without knowing it, he had carried this with him the whole time on his journey. And now he also realized that it had been his father's voice that spoke in his dreams.

As he was gazing in wonder, his father said, "Now look at the casket lid and see what is there." Now a new marvel met his eyes, for in the lid he saw the whole island kingdom, the very place where he had been king, in all its shapes and colors. Yes, all the people were there! And it was not just a picture, for they lived and moved as he watched. Even the old man, his trusted adviser, was there smiling at him; and his eyes spoke in a way that the heart could know.

His father smiled, too. "See what you have been carrying in your golden casket! You kept your father's house with you always. The more you carried it with love, the more it was able to help you. You have journeyed well! Now come back into your father's house. You must rest here a while before I send you out on another journey."

9

More Stories that Help Children with Loss

In working with children who have experienced loss, parents and teachers need to take into account child development. In Portland, Oregon, The Dougy Center for Grieving Children published a small publication, *35 Ways to Help a Grieving Child*. They concisely present helpful tips born of many years of work with support groups and various activities at their center. Under heading "#30" they state, "Understand that grief looks different at different ages" (Dougy Center, p. 36).

For example, "When five-year-old Nancy saw her deceased father's car in the driveway for the first time since he died, she asked her mother, 'Is Daddy home?' Her older sister Kara replied, 'Of course not, Daddy died a month ago'" (ibid., p. 36). Many young children struggle to understand the finality of death and as with Nancy, can expect that the lost parent will return. Often they use play as the medium for expressing their grief and remembering the loved one who has departed.

Older children may ask more detailed questions about death and can engage in more conversation. Yet even as they grow older, there may still be times when they "act out" to get attention to their needs. The Dougy Center and other such organizations are dedicated to providing that support, often through group activities.

Teens will increasingly turn to their peers for support given "the natural egocentrism that accompanies adolescence" (ibid., p. 36). They may become absorbed in their personal emotional response to a death and question the meaning of life and the "why" of death. As children grow older, they often revisit their grief, sometimes attaching new meaning to the loss. "Seventeen year-old Rita, whose mother died of cancer when she was 6, said she began missing her mom in a new way when she entered high school. 'I was feeling sad and lonely. At first I thought it was just because I was in a new school. But I think now it's because I missed having a mom I could share my feelings with'" (ibid., p. 36).

I found it interesting that in another section of the literature, the Dougy Center describes how some kids act younger than their age after a death. Their anxiety and insecurity can lead to behaviors of younger children, such as wanting to sleep in a parent's bed, throwing tantrums or reverting to bed-wetting. Rather than punishment, children need time to return to their higher functioning behaviors as they learn to cope with their grief.

The role of parents, teachers and counselors is crucial in all these stages. Rather than just helping children "get over it," we need to validate their feelings by listening, talking and supporting in age-appropriate ways. Children are impacted by a loss throughout their life span, and how they experience grief and process their feelings will affect many other aspects of emotional development and future relationships.

In a Waldorf school and in homes influenced by that pedagogy, a tremendous resource can be found in age-appropriate stories. Of course it is best when they are told rather than read, but a carefully chosen story can heal on many levels. I remember so well having one of my children at my side on the sofa or a big leather recliner as I did the bedtime stories over the years. There is a sense of comfort, warmth and security that comes just in the proximity to one another. Then there is the story itself, which can speak to a child through images and character development. Rather than preaching, the meaning of a good story can be grasped at the level a child needs to hear, and other parts may be overlooked for good reason. Our children are wise beyond the recognition of many in today's world. Finally, there are opportunities after the story or the next day to respond to a child's question or request for a brief chat. Rather than "explaining," I often found that a simple affirmation or retelling could support the observation the child chose to make. This builds inner certainty that the world is imbued with wisdom and meaning, and that good can come from pain and struggle.

Even an interruption in the reading of a story can be significant. There may well be a reason why a child makes an exclamation at one point in the narrative, or asks a question. Again, I found less is more—affirmation, a simple response, and then resumption of the tale. When children want to discuss something further, they will say so. All too often, adults go into unsolicited "explanations" that can actually diminish the depth and meaning of the narrative. Stories are often far more wise than we are!

Below are a few examples of stories with some indicators for age-appropriateness. Most of all, parents and teachers need to use their common sense and exercise their loving intuition as to which story to tell and when. No two children are exactly alike, and what works for one may not work for another. These stories focus particularly on processing death and building an inner imaginative transformation. The first one comes from Patricia Carlin at the New Amsterdam School, and it is ideal for kindergarten and the very young child.

A Story for Finny and Theoa

Once there was a beautiful willow tree that lived in the garden. All the schoolchildren loved to visit the willow tree and even called her "Mrs. Willow." The willow tree liked that name! Mrs. Willow was very friendly and generous; the children loved making willow crowns with the feathery branches that Mrs. Willow let fall to the ground.

When the birds asked if they could make nests in her branches, Mrs. Willow said, "Yes, of course; it's my pleasure!"

When the squirrels asked if they could make nests in her branches, Mrs. Willow said, "Yes, of course; it's pleasure!"

When the butterflies asked if they could play in her branches, Mrs. Willow said, "Yes, of course, with pleasure!"

And so, the butterflies moved in. When they walked with their tiny, delicate feet on Mrs. Willow's branches, she said, "It tickles!"

But most of all, Mrs. Willow loved watching the butterfly friends play with one another, for each one was good and kind. Sometimes, in their games, the butterflies made tiny houses with twigs and berries on

Mrs. Willow's branches. Sometimes, one or two of the butterflies would be "baby butterflies," and the others would be the mommy, daddy, sister, and brother butterflies. Two of the butterflies who had the speediest wings would race around Mrs. Willow's long branches, flying so fast and laughing and laughing. All of the butterfly friends were very happy, and Mrs. Willow was happy too.

One day, a new little butterfly friend arrived at the tree. He was very gentle and watched all of the other butterflies playing. Mrs. Willow was watching too and said, "Come, gentle butterfly, and play with all the butterfly friends." The butterfly friends said, "Yes, please play with us, gentle butterfly." And so he did. And he was happy.

Shortly after, a big, loud storm threw many raindrops to the earth. Mrs. Willow called all the butterfly friends to huddle under her leafy umbrellas to stay dry. As the butterflies looked out at the storm together, each one held the wing of the other, to protect and comfort one another.

In a while, the big storm was over and the bright sun appeared once again in the sky. But some of the raindrops still hovered in the sky, and when the bright sunlight shone through them, a marvelous rainbow appeared. The butterflies, who loved colors of all shades, were enchanted. As they watched, a second rainbow appeared, and the whole sky was bursting with colors. The butterflies were even more enchanted. One of them said, "Let's fly to the rainbows and dive into the colors!" One by one, they launched themselves upward, saying, "Goodbye, Mrs. Willow! We'll be back soon!"

But it is not so easy to fly to a rainbow, for it is very far away in the sky. One by one, the delicate wings of each butterfly grew tired, and most of the butterflies turned around and flew wearily back to Mrs. Willow. But not the gentle butterfly; he flew all the way to the rainbow, and it was so beautiful and its colors were so grand that he decided to stay in the rainbow. When he opened his wings, they became glorious rainbow wings, and he became the rainbow butterfly.

All the Willow butterfly friends missed their friend, the gentle butterfly, and wished that he would come again and play with them. And whenever they saw a rainbow, they remembered with love their gentle friend.

And if they looked very carefully, they really could see their gentle friend inside the rainbow, shining in all light and goodness onto the world.

The Three Snake-Leaves

Grimm brothers (suitable for five- and six-year-olds)

There was once on a time a poor man, who could no longer support his only son. Then said the son, "Dear father, things go so badly with us that I am a burden to you. I would rather go away and see how I can earn my bread." So the father gave him his blessing, and with great sorrow took leave of him. At this time the King of a mighty empire was at war, and the youth took service with him, and went out to fight. And when he came before the enemy, there was a battle, and great danger, and it rained shot until his comrades fell on all sides, and when the leader also was killed, those left were about to take flight, but the youth stepped forth, spoke boldly to them, and cried, "We will not let our fatherland be ruined!" Then the others followed him, and he pressed on and conquered the enemy. When the King heard that he owed the victory to him alone, he raised him above all the others, gave him great treasures, and made him the first in the kingdom.

This theme of rags to riches is often found in fairy tales from around the world; the simpleton or the person with no means is elevated to a position above others through a kind of divine "blessing." In this case, the hero showed remarkable courage, which is often associated with the human heart, a theme that will be borne out in further episodes of his life.

The King had a daughter who was very beautiful, but she was also very strange. She had made a vow to take no one as her lord and husband who did not promise to let himself be buried alive with her if she died first. "If he loves me with all his heart," said she, "of what use will life be to him afterward?" On her side she would do the same, and if he died first, would go down to the grave with him. This strange oath had up to this time frightened away all wooers, but the youth became so charmed with her beauty that he cared for nothing, but asked her father for her. "But do you know what you must promise?" said the King. "I must be buried with her," he replied, "if I outlive her, but my love is so great that I do not mind the danger." Then the King consented, and the wedding was solemnized with great splendor.

Male and female roles in these stories should not be considered from a modern-day view of sex and gender. Rather, in the spirit of Jung, they often portray two aspects of the human soul that seek unification. We all have a male and a female side within our soul (anima and animus) and the narrative describes the journey toward unification. In this case, the ideal is set very high; the "strange oath" that if one should die, the other would follow, perhaps the ultimate vow of fidelity.

For young children faced with a death in the family or school, this begins to work with a deep-seated question that resides in us all: Will we be faithful, make the ultimate pledge of commitment? Will my Mom or Dad remarry? Does marriage/partnership continue beyond the grave? In hinting that it does, the tale also opens the false door a crack to the notion that there may be life after death.

> They lived now for a while happy and contented with each other, and then it befell that the young Queen was attacked by a severe illness, and no physician could save her. And as she lay there dead, the young King remembered what he had been obliged to promise, and was horrified at having to lie down alive in the grave, but there was no escape. The King had placed sentries at all the gates, and it was not possible to avoid his fate. As the day came when the corpse was to be buried, he was taken down with it into the royal vault and then the door was shut and bolted.

They lived happily just for a while. Are we to take this literally in terms of months or years, or should we continue the preceding thought? Is our time on Earth "for just a while"? We cannot know for sure, but illness and death strike us all at some point, so the question is put to the test: Do our resolves in life carry over into death?

> Near the coffin stood a table on which were four candles, four loaves of bread, and four bottles of wine, and when this provision came to an end, he would have to die of hunger.

Another riddle: Why four? Is this arbitrary, as so much today seems at first glance, or is there meaning that goes beyond the number and hard, cold facts? I am not sure. When working with groups of adults, I try to assist the discovery process, rather than give answers. And with children, the less said about these things the better. Too much today is "explained" and rationalized already. So perhaps in the recall or remembering of the story in the days after, one can put the simple question: How many and why? Is that all the king had to offer? How long can one live on the Earth without eating or drinking? For adult consideration, one can see a possibility of the fourfold human being that needs nourishment to stay "present" on the Earth—the physical; the etheric, or life force; the astral, or our varying states of consciousness; the self-aware "I," or self. Rationing the four loaves and bottle of wine takes special effort by the astral, a challenge for all who struggle for control and mastery of self.

> And now he sat there full of pain and grief, ate every day only a little piece of bread, drank only a mouthful of wine, and nevertheless saw death daily drawing nearer. Whilst he thus gazed before him, he saw a snake creep out of a corner of the vault and approach the dead body. And as he thought it came to gnaw at it, he drew his sword and said, "As long as I live, you shall not touch her," and hewed the snake in three pieces. After a time a second snake crept out of the hole, and when it saw the other lying dead and cut in pieces, it went back, but soon came again with three green leaves in its mouth. Then it took the three pieces of the snake, laid them together, as they fitted, and placed one of the leaves on each wound. Immediately the severed parts joined themselves together, the snake moved and became alive again, and both of them hastened away together. The leaves were left lying on the ground, and a desire came into the mind of the unhappy man who had been watching all this, to know if the wondrous power of the leaves that had brought the snake to life again, could not likewise be of service to a human being. So he picked up the leaves and laid one of them on the mouth of his dead wife, and the two others on her eyes. And hardly had he done this than the blood stirred in her veins, rose into her pale face, and colored it again. Then she drew breath, opened her eyes, and said, "Ah, God, where am I?" "You are with me, dear wife," he answered, and told her how everything had happened, and how he had brought her back again to life. Then he gave her some wine and bread, and when she had regained her strength, he raised her up and they went to the door and knocked,

and called so loudly that the sentries heard it, and told the King. The King came down himself and opened the door, and there he found both strong and well, and rejoiced with them that now all sorrow was over. The young King, however, took the three snake-leaves with him, gave them to a servant and said, "Keep them for me carefully, and carry them constantly about you; who knows in what trouble they may yet be of service to us!"

More riddles! Why a snake? What kind of magical leaves could these be? Why are they placed on the eyes and mouth? Some things cannot be fully known, and it helps if the parent or teacher holds inner questions without verbalizing them with children, knowing that there is so much more in a good story than one can realize at first. This inner "holding" is a spiritual act, one that nourishes the potency of meaning and helps the storyteller be alive and active with the content. There is so much in the world today that is dead-ended. We need to open inquiry and entertain thoughts for which there is no instant answer.

Having said all this, the passage above goes to the heart of the story, death and resurrection. Both the initial snake and the wife are brought back to life, thanks to the leaves. Many young children want to know if someone "will come back again"; the story plays this out through pictures. Yet as we soon hear, a "return" is not that simple:

> But a change had taken place in his wife; after she had been restored to life, it seemed as if all love for her husband had gone out of her heart. After some time, when he wanted to make a voyage over the sea, to visit his old father, and they had gone on board a ship, she forgot the great love and fidelity that he had shown her, and that had been the means of rescuing her from death, and conceived a wicked inclination for the skipper. And once when the King lay there asleep, she called in the skipper and seized the sleeper by the head, and the skipper took him by the feet, and thus they threw him down into the sea. When the shameful deed was done, she said, "Now let us return home, and say that he died on the way. I will extol and praise you so to my father that he will marry me to you, and make you the heir to his crown." But the faithful servant who had seen all that they did, unseen by them, unfastened a little boat from the ship, got into it, sailed after his master, and let the traitors go on their way. He fished up the dead body, and by the help of the three snake-leaves that he

carried about with him, and laid on the eyes and mouth, he fortunately brought the young King back to life.

Betrayal is a kind of death, which now occurs again, this time in the slaying of the husband. Yet juxtaposed with this horrid deed, we have the faithfulness of the servant/friend who has guarded the snake leaves all this time. Why did the wife change so much? It is hard to answer that question on the basis of physical laws, so I suspect the wisdom of the fairy tale points to the larger reality we can call reincarnation. When we return, we are different, both in personality and in terms of new relationships. The ocean waters carry us in and out of life.

> They both rowed with all their strength day and night, and their little boat sailed so swiftly that they reached the old King before the others. He was astonished when he saw them come alone, and asked what had happened to them. When he learnt the wickedness of his daughter he said, "I cannot believe that she has behaved so ill, but the truth will soon come to light," and bade both go into a secret chamber and keep themselves hidden from everyone. Soon afterward, the great ship came sailing in, and the godless woman appeared before her father with a troubled countenance. He said, "Why do you come back alone? Where is your husband?" "Ah, dear father," she replied, "I come home again in great grief; during the voyage, my husband became suddenly ill and died, and if the good skipper had not given me his help, it would have gone ill with me. He was present at his death, and can tell you all." The King said, "I will make the dead alive again," and opened the chamber, and bade the two come out. When the woman saw her husband, she was thunderstruck, and fell on her knees and begged for mercy. The King said, "There is no mercy. He was ready to die with you and restored you to life again, but you have murdered him in his sleep, and shall receive the reward that you deserve." Then she was placed with her accomplice in a ship that had been pierced with holes, and sent out to sea, where they soon sank amid the waves.

Many world religions have various laws of justice, some more harsh than others. But this is more than infidelity. The words "I will make the dead alive again" are spoken by the king, who has ruled the kingdom all the time, just as our Self rules over our own conduct in life. It is the inner rulership of the I that can ultimately effect change in human conduct.

Sometimes parents have objected to the violent endings of some of these tales, wanting to spare their children from graphic images of sinking in a ship pierced with holes. The protective gesture of a parent is understandable. Yet we live in a world in which children are exposed all too soon to much worse in video games and movies. The difference between these instances and a story told by a living parent or teacher is that there is a big difference between imposing images from without or leaving things up to the imagination of the child. Over the years I have found that young children both hear and imagine what they need, and in pictures that are self-created and mobile, whereas the images that bombard the senses from without are fixed and already fully shaped by others. Forcing oneself on others is a root characteristic of violence, much more so than telling a story. In fact, some exposure to self-created images can help build character and the ability to discern that serves our children well later in life.

So as we see in the above story and in many others, death is not final, but rather a stage in a larger cycle. Without death we could not have life, as seen in an African Asante myth:

> Although people did not like the idea or experience of death, they nevertheless embraced it when given the choice, as in the tale of an ancient people who, upon experiencing their first visitation of death, pleaded with God to stop it. God granted this wish, and for three years there was no death. But there were also no births during that time. Unwilling to endure this absence of children, the people beseeched God to return death to them as long as they could have children again.*

At the same time I read this story, I noticed a piece in the news about declining birth rates all over the world. In a few years, in practically all countries except some in Africa, our population will be shrinking. This is not the place to debate environmental and population issues, but for a teacher and parent, the phrase "unwilling to endure the absence of children" is poignant. What would our world be like without children, who

---

* See http://www.deathreference.com/Ho-Ka/How-Death-Came-into-the-World.html#ixzz5GirQsmHf.

in themselves represent renewal and hope? Why is our world becoming less hospitable for children?

In keeping with the theme of death as transformation, there are many stories in which the human form is changed. This has the effect of "opening" our concept of death to wider horizons, as described literally in the tale "The Seven Ravens":

> There was once a man who had seven sons, and still he had no daughter, however much he wished for one. At length his wife again gave him hope of a child, and when it came into the world it was a girl. The joy was great, but the child was sickly and small, and had to be privately baptized on account of its weakness. The father sent one of the boys in haste to the spring to fetch water for the baptism. The other six went with him, and as each of them wanted to be first to fill it, the jug fell into the well. There they stood and did not know what to do, and none of them dared to go home. As they still did not return, the father grew impatient and said, "They have certainly forgotten it while playing some game, the wicked boys!" He became afraid that the girl would have to die without being baptized, and in his anger cried, "I wish the boys were all turned into ravens." Hardly were these words spoken before he heard a whirring of wings over his head, looked up, and saw seven coal-black ravens flying away. (Grimm, 1944, p. 137)

The daughter survived and grew to be a beautiful girl, but upon discovering the fate of her brothers, set out to find them. She had to travel to the end of the world (one way of describing death) and visited the sun, moon and stars, asking for help. With the help of cosmic wisdom, she was able to find her way to the Glass Mountain, but had to sacrifice her little finger to unlock the door. One inside, she prepared to surprise her raven brothers by dropping her parent's ring into one of their glasses, and upon finding it, the ravens were changed back to brothers. This is a beautiful example of the journey between worlds, the devotion of the "sister" left behind, and the release of a spell through the power of the ring, what binds all in a symbol of unity.

Children who are told such stories grow up with living images of the world beyond the Earth, and when a brother or sister is lost, can be reminded of the journey beyond our everyday world of the senses. These stories build security and confidence in divine goodness.

The narrative is not so pleasing in another tale from the brothers Grimm, that of the Godfather Death, which might not be told until children are seven or eight:

> Once upon a time there was a poor tailor who could barely feed his twelve children. When the thirteenth was born, the distraught man ran out to the road nearby determined to find someone to stand as godfather to the child. He knew of no other way that he could provide for his newborn son. The first person to pass was God, but the poor tailor rejected him. "God gives to the rich and takes from the poor. I'll wait for another to come." The second to pass was the Devil, but the poor tailor rejected him, too. "He lies and cheats and leads good men astray. I'll wait for another." The third man to pass was Death, and the poor tailor considered him carefully. "Death treats all men alike, whether rich or poor. He's the one I'll ask."
>
> Now Death had never been asked such a thing before, but he agreed at once. "Your child shall lack for nothing," he said, "for I am a powerful friend indeed." The years went by and he kept his word. The boy and his family lacked for nothing. When the boy finally came of age, his Godfather Death appeared before him. "It is time to establish you in the world. You are to become a great physician. Take this magical herb, the cure for any malady of this Earth. Look for me when you're called to a patient's bed. If you see me at its head then give them a tincture of the herb and your patient will be well. But if you see me at the foot, you'll know it is their time to die. Your diagnosis will always be right, and you will be famous around the world.
>
> And so it was. The young man became the most famous doctor of his time, and his fame spread far and wide until it reached the ears of the king. The king lay sick in his golden bed and he summoned the tailor's son to him. But when the young doctor arrived at last in the richly appointed bedchamber, he saw that the king was gravely ill and that Death stood at his feet. Now this king was much beloved and the young man wanted to cure him very much. He quickly instructed the court attendants to turn the bed the opposite way, and he then restored the king to health with a tincture of the magical herb. Death was not pleased. He shook his long, bony finger at his godson and said, "You must never cheat me again. If you do, it will be the worse for you."
>
> The young man took this warning to heart and did not cross his godfather again—until the king's daughter fell ill and he was

summoned back to the palace. This was the good king's only child. He was desperate to see her well. "Save her life," said the king, "I shall give you her hand in marriage." The doctor went to the lovely maiden's bedchamber, where Death was waiting. He stood at the foot of the princess's bed, ready to take her away. "Don't cross me again," his godfather warned, but the doctor was half in love already. He ordered the princess's bed to be turned and he gave her the herbal tincture.

The princess was healed immediately, but Death reached out a cold, white hand and clamped it on his godson's arm, saying. "You'll go with me instead." He took the young man into a cave, its wall niches covered with millions of candles. "Here," he said, "are candles burning for every life upon the Earth. Each time a candle grows low and snuffs out, a life is ended. This one is yours." Death pointed to a candle that had burned down to a pool of wax. "Please," his godson begged, "for many years I was your faithful servant. Please, Godfather Death, won't you light a new candle for me?" Death gazed at him remorselessly. The candle sputtered and flickered out. The young doctor fell down dead.*

For children in second grade, one might tell the biography of St. Elizabeth Ann Seton, the patron saint of death and grief. Having experienced it multiple times in her life, from her mother to her husband to two of her five children, she sought a more intimate relationship to God. In her journey, she lost her health and social standing, even becoming ostracized in her community. Yet her story gives a picture of inner resilience and has American roots (New York City).

For third grade, as the children start to become more conscious of themselves as distinct from their environment, they need to find a new relationship to authority. In the case of the following African myth, authority is represented by Old Old One. Yet the chameleon and the lizard have two very different responses and messages regarding life and death. Stories of this pattern are widespread in Africa especially among tribes belonging to the great Bantu family, which occupies roughly the southern half of the continent. The best-known example of the tale is the one told by the Zulus.

---

* See http://www.terriwindling.com/blog/2016/10/death-in-fairytales.html.

They say that in the beginning Unkulunkulu, that is the Old Old One, sent the chameleon to men with a message saying "Go chameleon, go and say Let not men die." The chameleon set out, but it crawled very slowly and it loitered by the way to eat the purple berries of the ubukwebezane tree, or according to others it climbed up a tree to bask in the sun, filled its belly with flies, and fell fast asleep. Meantime the Old Old One had thought better of it and sent a lizard posting after the chameleon with a very different message to men, for he said to the animal, "Lizard, when you have arrived, say Let men die." So the lizard went on his way, passed the dawdling chameleon, and arriving first among men delivered his message of death saying "Let men die." Then he turned on his heel and went back to the Old Old One who had sent him. But after he was gone, the chameleon at last arrived among men with his glad tidings of immortality, and he shouted saying, "It is said Let not men die!" But men answered "O! we have heard the word of the lizard; it has told us the word 'It is said Let men die.' We cannot hear your word. Through the word of the lizard men will die." And died they have ever since, from that day to this. That is why some of the Zulus hate the lizard, saying "Why did he run first and say 'Let people die?'" So they beat and kill the lizard and say "Why did it speak?" But others hate the chameleon and hustle it, saying "That is the little thing that delayed to tell the people that they should not die. If he had only brought his message in time we should not have died; our ancestors also would have been still living; there would have been no diseases here on the Earth. It all comes from the delay of the chameleon."

The same story is told in nearly the same form by other Bantu tribes such as the Bechuanas, the Basutos, the Baronga and the Ngoni. To this day the Baronga and the Ngoni owe the chameleon a grudge for having brought death into the world, so when children find a chameleon they will induce it to open its mouth then throw a pinch of tobacco on its tongue and watch with delight the creature writhing and changing colour from orange to green, from green to black, in the agony of death; for thus they avenge the wrong that the chameleon has done to humankind.*

In this story, we see how animals can often represent very human characteristics, thus continuing the pattern of the other stories in which imagination helps to paint a full landscape. Children at age nine are moving from a view of one whole world to that of greater differentiation.

---

* See https://www.giffordlectures.org/books/belief-immortality-and-worship-dead/lecture-3-myths-origin-death.

They are ready to see that there are consequences to our actions, and that the indolence of the chameleon resulted in the possibility of diseases and even death. Even the idea of a grudge is a human trait, as is the cruel treatment of the chameleon as an example of revenge. The possibility of death serves to awaken human consciousness.

Third-graders in a Waldorf schools also learn about Genesis, which speaks further about their gradual awakening:

> Adam and Eve thus "fall" into the flesh, into the world as it is known, with the entire legacy that embodiment entails: work, suffering, and physical death. Paradoxically, the Tree of Knowledge heralds ignorance of their divine nature, and the fall into flesh signals their sleepwalking indifference to that nature. Human beings therefore need God's help through the divine mercy of his Son or the sacred texts of the Bible to awaken them to their divine destiny. Without this awakening, the wages of sin are eternal death—an eternal darkness spent in chains of ignorance, a blindness maintained by humans' attachment to mere earthly concerns and distractions. This famous story thus embodies all the paradoxical elements of creation, implying that human life is actually no life at all, but its opposite: death.*

When I was a child, my mother read stories each night, some from her old, worn edition of Grimms. She had a habit of paging through the book to find a suitable story for the evening, but whenever she came to The Juniper Tree, she would say "This is too sad to read"...so I never heard it! Years later as a teacher, I came to the same conclusion and never told it in class. Strangely enough, although it is all about death, as I went through this chapter I decided to place it in the appendix rather than here. It is also a real question as to where it might fit, age-wise, in the curriculum. So this is the teaser...see appendix if wanted.

For fourth grade, many Waldorf teachers tell the Norse story of Baldur. See the separate chapter with my favorite version.

In fifth grade, the theme of death through stories could return in telling of Cupid:

---

* See http://www.deathreference.com/Ho-Ka/How-Death-Came-into-the-World.html#ixzz5Gis4u4q9.

Cupid, one sultry summer's noon, tired with play and faint with heat, went into a cool grotto to repose himself. This happened to be the cave of Death. He threw himself carelessly down upon the floor, and his quiver turning upside down, all the arrows fell out, and mingled with those of Death, which lay scattered about the place. When he awoke, he gathered them up as well as he could; but they were so intermingled, that although he knew the proper number to take, he could not rightly distinguish his own. Hence he took up some of the arrows that belonged to Death, and left some of his. This is the cause that we now and then see the hearts of the old and decrepit transfixed with the bolts of Love; and with great grief and surprise, sometimes see youth and beauty smitten with the darts of Death.*

When learning about the myths and culture of ancient India, children can be introduced to the life and teachings of Buddha. The story below shows the inevitability of death and the importance of acceptance of both life and death:

Buddha was staying in a village. A woman came to him, weeping and crying and screaming. Her child, her only child, had suddenly died. Because Buddha was in the village, people said, "Don't weep. Go to this man. People say he is infinite compassion. If he wills it, the child can revive. So don't weep. Go to this Buddha." The woman came with the dead child, crying, weeping, and the whole village followed her—the whole village was affected. Buddha's disciples were also affected; they started praying in their minds that Buddha would have compassion. He must bless the child so that he will be revived, resurrected.

Many disciples of Buddha started weeping. The scene was so touching, deeply moving. Everybody was still. Buddha remained silent. He looked at the dead child, then he looked at the weeping, crying mother and he said to the mother, "Don't weep, just do one thing and your child will be alive again. Leave this dead child here, go back to the town, go to every house and ask every family if someone has ever died in their family, in their house. And if you can find a house where no one has ever died, then from them beg something to be eaten, some bread, some rice, or anything—but from the house where no one has ever died. And that bread or that rice will revive the child immediately. You go. Don't waste time."

The woman became happy. She felt that now the miracle was going to happen. She touched Buddha's feet and ran to the village,

---

* See https://fablesofaesop.com/death-cupid.html.

which was not a very big one, very few cottages, a few families. She moved from one family to another, asking. But every family said, "This is impossible. There is not a single house—not only in this village but all over the Earth—there is not a single house where no one has ever died, where people have not suffered death and the misery and the pain and the anguish that comes out of it."

By and by the woman realized that Buddha had been playing a trick. This was impossible. But still the hope was there. She went on asking until she had gone around the whole village. Her tears dried, her hope died, but suddenly she felt a new tranquility, a serenity, coming to her. Now she realized that whosoever is born will have to die. It is only a question of years. Someone will die sooner, someone later, but death is inevitable. She came back and touched Buddha's feet again and said to him, "As people say, you really do have a deep compassion for people." (OSHO)

There are many other opportunities in fifth grade, such as when telling the story of Perseus and how he encounters Medusa. Her very glance can turn a person into stone! Thus he is instructed to look only at her reflected image in his shiny shield when seeking to slay her...a wonderful link between the formation of a concept and the death process. When one looks directly, as in a percept, one is united with the world. But in order to form a concept one has, so to speak, to "turn away" from direct perception. This is intimately connected with our nerve-sense system, more of which is explained in the chapter on life and death. But for fifth graders, the dawning of conceptual abilities coincides nicely with the story of Perseus and Medusa.

The history curriculum in Waldorf sixth to eighth grades is filled with opportunities for class discussion of struggle, hopes, dreams and life/death issues. One cannot list them all here. But I would like to draw the reader's attention to another story included in the appendix that might fit with a lesson segment on coal mining and the early Industrial Revolution, as brought in eighth grade.

"The Odor of Chrysanthemums" by D. H. Lawrence can be a valuable part of English literature when teaching allegory, foreshadowing, atmosphere, and symbolism...but for teachers looking at the subject of death, a crucial paragraph appears near the end of the story, when the dead miner is brought home to his wife and she stands in the parlor looking at him:

> The eyes, half shut, did not show glazed in the obscurity. Life with its smoky burning gone from him, had left him apart and utterly alien to her. And she knew what a stranger he was to her. In her womb was ice of fear, because of this separate stranger with whom she had been living as one flesh. Was this what it all meant—utter, intact separateness, obscured by heat of living? In dread she turned her face away. The fact was too deadly. There had been nothing between them, and yet they had come together, exchanging their nakedness repeatedly. Each time he had taken her, they had been two isolated beings, far apart as now. He was no more responsible than she. The child was like ice in her womb. For as she looked at the dead man, her mind, cold and detached, said clearly, "Who am I? What have I been doing? I have been fighting a husband who did not exist. HE existed all the time. What wrong have I done? What was that I have been living with? There lies the reality, this man." And her soul died in her for fear; she knew she had never seen him, he had never seen her, they had met in the dark and had fought in the dark, not knowing whom they met nor whom they fought. And now she saw, and turned silent in seeing. For she had been wrong. She had said he was something he was not; she had felt familiar with him. Whereas he was apart all the while, living as she never lived, feeling as she never felt.
>
> In fear and shame she looked at his naked body, that she had known falsely. And he was the father of her children. Her soul was torn from her body and stood apart. She looked at his naked body and was ashamed, as if she had denied it. After all, it was itself. It seemed awful to her. She looked at his face, and she turned her own face to the wall. For his look was other than hers, his way was not her way. She had denied him what he was—she saw it now. She had refused him as himself. And this had been her life, and his life. She was grateful to death, which restored the truth. And she knew she was not dead.*

This might be more suitable for high school, but when a teacher has been with a class for many years through the elementary school, one can sometimes take risks, and this may be one such instance for an eighth grade. The themes that can be drawn out in class discussion include:

---

* See https://ebooks.adelaide.edu.au/l/lawrence/dh/l410.

1. Separation: when were husband and wife most separate and when are they "together"?
2. How has she changed from the beginning of the story to the end?
3. Why was she ashamed?
4. Why was she grateful for death?

Teachers need to make choices on a daily basis, but it is far better to do this in the classroom than in publishing houses and/or based on state standards. The questions one asks in class should arise from a direct perception of the needs of the students and what is possible on a given day. When successful, a good story can speak to larger archetypes that are eternal, ones that can serve for years to come. When told in an age-appropriate manner, stories can build character and inner resilience.

10

Adolescent Boys and Death

Since I wrote *Education for Nonviolence,* the chapter on boys has elicited many responses. From the questions I receive after giving talks, it is clear that the topic of boys in general has resonated with many, but also raised questions that beg further discussion. It is not just because young men are often behind mass-shooting incidents in schools and elsewhere, thus drawing forth our attention, but also because in some classrooms it is boys who receive the most reprimands and seem less willing to conform to "expectations." Any stereotyping is wrong, but when it comes to gender issues, it seems there is less consciousness than there should be. All too often boys are perceived as "acting out," and, as a result, the perceptions of some adults are trained to look for such behavior.

When boys have role models that exemplify the "silent male" and decline to express themselves verbally, it has implications for how emotions can be processed. Things can be bottled up and fester over time. Of course there are some who grow up in homes that put a high emphasis on conversation, and those that go to good schools do learn to banter, negotiate and share thoughts and feelings. But not all children are so fortunate, and verbal skills all too often are influenced by family income, geographic location of a school and other attributes of entitlement.

Thus I returned to the book by Celia Lashlie, *He'll be OK: Growing Gorgeous Boys into Good Men,* and found a remarkable dialogue with boys on the subject of death:

> It was very common in the course of my visits to find myself at a school that was mourning the loss of a student or a recent graduate, either through suicide or death on the road. As I watched the schools

grapple with the situation time and again, I became aware that the reality of death sits very close to the lives of boys, possibly a lot closer than it did for people of my generation. A significant number of young men are taking the option of suicide or are driving themselves and their mates to death or injury on the roads and as a result adolescent boys are feeling deep and painful emotions as a part of their everyday lives, even if they don't appear to be affected. It was during my discussions with Year 13 students about suicide, death and grief that the window was open on their natural wisdom (Lashlie, p.138).

"Who has had someone close to them die?"
Several of them put up their hands.
"Can someone give me a visual image of their grief?"
There was no pause at all before one student leapt up saying, as he cupped his hands together, "Mine's a small hard ball."
"And you're holding it right now?"
"Yeah."
"So it fits in your hand?"
"Yep."
"OK, now you've got it in your hand, what do you do with it?"
"I put it down here and go over there and play a game."
"Does the game involve physical contact?"
"Yep, the harder the better."
"So you've played the game. Now you look back toward the grief. Had it changed shape?"
"No."
"Will anything make it smaller?"
"No."
"Talking?"
"No!"
"So it just stays that size?"
"Yeah."
'Permanently?"
"Time might make a difference."
"But it will be a part of who you are forever?"
"Yep."
The boy next to him picked up the image.
"Miss, mine's not a ball," He said. "I know it's a cliche but mine's a bottle—I put grief in the bottle and screw the top down."
"Does the bottle ever get full?"
"Yep."
"What do you do with it?"
At this point, he made as if to throw something over his shoulder.

"Does it hit someone?"

"Yeah, usually." (ibid., p. 140)

Both of them, you'll notice, talk about physical contact (in one case, the harder the better) as a way of coping with grief.

Another boy then joined in. "Mine's a bottle, too, Miss, but I don't ever have to throw mine away. I've got a hole drilled into the bottom and it drips away at a pace I can cope with." (ibid.)

His neighbor added, "I've got a bottle, too, Miss, and it's got one of those cords"—he was miming an intensive care drip—"and I can move the clip as necessary to increase or lessen the flow." (ibid.)

The use of imagery to deal with heavy emotions is striking, as is the intensity of feeling behind them. These boys in New Zealand were clearly struggling to process their emotions and experiences of death.

Whereas younger children might receive solace and some opportunity to process death experiences through stories as indicated in another chapter, these adolescent boys clearly benefited from dialogue. It remains for parents and teachers to ask themselves: How can we provide such opportunities when needed? Rather than just placing more metal detectors in schools and arming teachers, perhaps we need to look at curriculum through a new lens. And for both boys and girls, we need to build resiliency that can help them deal with the inevitable hard knocks of life.

11

The Open Door

Karine Munk Finser

When Gilgamesh set out to overcome death, only to experience its finiteness, he was inspired by the sorrow of loss. The dark ocean of separation by the death of a loved one would know no comfort, were it not for the accompanying sun-like rays that can be absorbed and when tended regularly, have the capacity to transform a life. We've often seen it; the grumpy person whom everyone feared, gradually softening and becoming lovable after the death of a partner. An older person, suddenly alone after fifty years' marriage and forced to develop new ways of living, re-finds themselves in their eighties, doing all the things they never thought possible. The list goes on. There is no denying these stories that we hold, which bring unexpected new aspects into the collective family history, in which biographies and traditions mingle.

As we know, there are many ways of leaving this earthly realm, and sometimes we can see the signature of the individual's life clearly portrayed in the last hours or days. If we are privileged to sit by the side of a dear one's departure, there is a distinct experience and unique quality of waiting. This mystery-waiting connects us with our entire spiritual ancestry. The doors of the heart and the doors of the spirit become one great big passage; we realize in that moment that all live within one another, and that the heart is not only our home but also the fiery doorway that we will pass through one day, into a place that we cannot fathom, but that can allow for these worlds to intermingle, undeniably changing a life forever.

Sometimes, there's no waiting granted, no sitting and seeing that life leave its body breath by breath, but death is like a thunderclap. The spirit-door, however, opens wide, and the soul can slip out quickly, the body falling away, and the expansiveness of the experience is polarized; the departed leaving into the wideness of expanded consciousness, and the people left behind going through the contractions of shock and trauma. There the golden rays of death may not be as graceful, but life for those left behind becomes a place of practicing living without, an inner journey of slowly integrating the gold that the heart has been able to reach for.

Still, in time, both experiences become unified; the beloved has departed, and life has forever changed. Crossword puzzles and pencils, shoes and slippers left behind never to be stepped into again, handwritten notes and books, last signatures, and much-loved clothing, cherished objects, all echo a life and seem to fall like leaves from trees, standing in rows on tables and floor, to be chosen by family members. Sometimes shadows enter here, for all becomes revealed in the light of the death passage, when the hearts fly open and hindrances may reveal themselves. The new spiritual glue that will forever link us to our loved one is born from open-heartedness, from the fire of longing, and the new wellspring of tears that remind of sudden hidden waterfalls of walks in the forest. Loud or tender, streaming, and gently flowing heavenward as steam.

What is it then—that quality of radiance, the comfort of Gilgamesh—that confirms that what has been created is forever?

I recently said goodbye to a great dame, a woman who was a superb musician and a powerhouse of an artist. When she played the piano at performances, often Brahms and Rachmaninoff, she literally lifted off her chair as she came down on the keys, powerfully expressive, and her radiance and oneness with the music she played brought tears to many of us tenderhearted listeners. She had in life and in music, a gutsiness that was unmistakable and a belly laugh to go with it. When she entered a room, her grand personality was palpable.

After her husband died, she slowly changed into an old woman, dementia set in slightly, she decided not to wear her teeth, and she slept on the sofa in her living room, with all her belongings in that one room. This became her home, containing all her memories. She continued to play on the piano, especially music she had composed in her youth. Her friends were her eyes and ears on the world. Caretakers were with her around the clock, and so the days turned into months and years. Her grandchildren brought her the content of their lives, and a new baby was brought to visit. She lived there in her living room, surrounded by photos of a long life lived and suffered, celebrated, and sublimated.

I would visit her infrequently, every time having to overcome her now sunken-in face, and her countenance so different from how I inwardly carried her. Yet, once in conversation, her charm and loveliness always returned, and at some point she would always say, "I've loved you ever since you stepped off that bus," and I knew she meant it. I loved her, too. My connection to her was from way back; I had been married to her son when I was only twenty years old, at a time when I had barely stepped out of my childhood. A few years later, I had lived in her home for several months with my small children and this encounter had become one of the more formative experiences of my life. These people were completely non-materialistic, fully devoted to music, and to people. Their friends and students were their family. My children were brought up in this lap of music, and their passionate devotion to classical music was a gift that I cherish, a foundation for art appreciation, the basis of beauty that can change lives from the inside.

And now I arrived to say a last goodbye. My daughter was by her side holding her hand for several weeks, sleeping on the sofa beside her grandmother's hospital bed, holding the traumatized little dog that she would later adopt.

When I entered, on the last day of her conscious life here on Earth, I looked into her transparent face surrounded by a halo of gray hair, lying on the pillow. She sat up a little and lit up with joy when she saw me. She put her hands out to catch my face, and I fell into her hands. She could no longer speak, but looked at me with a radiance that hit me like a bright light. With my face in her hands, and her face so incredibly beautiful, a veil lifted for a split second; I became the prodigal son (or rather daughter) falling into the embrace of the elder; my heart surrendered and

I sharply experienced the edge of my own shortcomings. I could feel how deeply I had squandered what I had received as gifts, tasting an inner potential, feeling an inner brightness. I could see the divine world with me within it, and I cried deep tears because I was inwardly completely alive and honest and as true as when I birthed my four children into this world. Her moment had become my moment as well. The generosity of this encounter baffled me long afterward.

Who is to know? Who is to know what we really mean to each other? Why we come into each other's orbits? Mothers, fathers, grandfathers, siblings, aunts, uncles, and friends, stepparents, and whole and half siblings; who is to say why we came to meet one another and who is more important? It's all about realizing that we are here for one another, and to grow our hearts, and to accompany each other through life's endlessly open and unanticipated paths.

The next time I arrived, she was no longer awake. And because there was no one else to do it, no one that had been requested, I took it upon myself to humbly give her what could be termed her last rites.

And after another day had gone by, she died, this grand dame. I arrived an hour or two after her passage. I entered the house with the caretakers on the threshold of the door, leaving, their job done. They were weeping, their lives transformed, caring for this woman for seven years, all the hours of the day, having witnessed all her stories, and having been instructed in the wisdom and lawfulness of classical music. Now they had to leave, a chapter closing behind them. And in the house was the body and the daughter and the little dog. And the greatest gift had been given by my child; she had sat and let her grandmother die a peaceful death, with candles and music and incessant loving presence. Her grandmother could leave this world feeling safe and not alone.

And the friends arrived. Later the coroners. And my child and the friends went to another room, where they kept a quiet vigil and spoke words I will never know, while I watched the body be placed and a door to the porch wrenched open. A door that had never been opened in all the years I had known that house. I hadn't even noticed it. Now it was torn open, and the coroners with the body, now in a purple brown bag, wheeled the trolley through that door, out over the wooden floor of the porch where we had eaten so many homemade dinners, through the garden that had been so loved, where a proud water garden still sat adorned with flowers, and past well-known trees that had grown from new or small to large, where raspberries and asparagus plants and annual vegetables had been grown, peas and squash, all was passed by, until we arrived at the open hearse. They placed her inside, and I, as the only follower, put my hand where I knew was her head. I blessed her with all the powers that were mine. And then the door shut. And I waved until she was no longer visible. An old ritual, often performed right there on that very spot, and now the last time.

Who is to say what comforted Gilgamesh? Maybe it was a stranger, or maybe a friend, or maybe it was the gold that descended like mist from the beloved, into his heart?

12

How to Stay Connected

For those who have lost a friend or family member, staying connected is a daily occupation. Sometimes it is painful, other times surprising and unexpected, but living with someone who has departed is ongoing for many. Having heard from people such as Scarlett Lewis who lost her son, Jesse, at Sandy Hook, the days, weeks, years after the tragedy can be full of unexpected turns. Those who have been down that path have much to share, and this chapter seeks to harvest some of their wisdom.

First of all, it helps when we have some relationship to the spiritual world, to God, or a meditation practice. If this is the case, there may well already be a sense that we are separated from the spiritual worlds only by our consciousness, not by space. How we attend is crucial. When the heart is cracked open through an unexpected death, or even, as in the case of my Mom, with a death that was expected, there is a vulnerability that allows for bridge building. The soul that is tender is more susceptible to communication and feeling connected with those who have departed.

When speaking at funeral services, Rudolf Steiner often sounded the theme of perceiving our community. In fact, those who are dead physically are part of a vast community that extends far beyond our comprehension. In Annie Kagan's book *The Afterlife of Billy Fingers: How My Bad-Boy Brother Proved to Me There's Life After Death*, she writes about her many communications with her departed brother. She is often startled to hear his voice speaking to her:

> I look through and see you. I know how sad you are about my death. *Sad* is too small a word. *Bereft* is more like it. But death isn't as serious as you think it is, honey. So far, it's very enjoyable. Couldn't

be better, really. Try not to take death too seriously. As a matter of fact, try not to take life too seriously. You'd enjoy yourself a lot more. That's one of the secrets of life. You want to know another secret? Saying goodbye isn't as serious as it seems either, because we will meet again. (p. 14)

Regardless of what one might believe is possible, and I read the first parts of Kagan's book with a degree of skepticism, there are descriptions in the communications of Billy that ring true. Take for example the notion that *"sad* is too small." So much is truly "small" when seen just from the earthly perspective. Staying connected calls on us to grow up and out to larger dimensions.

In *Nurturing Healing Love: A Mother's Journey of Hope and Forgiveness*, Scarlett Lewis shares communications from her son that are so numerous they are hard to dismiss. Finding a toy soldier in her bed days later, a drawing from her son done days before Sandy Hook that depicted himself with angel wings, balloons that floated upward at the funeral to form a heart shape in the sky...all are part of what she calls energies and messages on the path of sacred grieving. The stories, so well told by Scarlett, show again and again that the threshold of death is indeed a "false door," one that is open far wider than we imagine.

That passageway is particularly permeable at night when in sleep. Then we are particularly close to those who have departed. The thoughts and ideas that have passed through our consciousness during the day now become quite visible to the departed loved ones. Steiner says that it is not merely surprising but also "shattering to see how human souls in life between death and rebirth rush toward sleeping souls in search of the thoughts and ideas those sleeping souls contain" (Selg, p. 13). They need this content as we who are living need food. Our thoughts and feelings come alive at night and nourish the departed.

In past times it was easier for the departed souls to connect with us who remain on the Earth, but that connection has become more challenging; the panels of the "door" have become thicker with our increasing focus on material things. Thus it is ever more important for us to read to the dead, send them our love, and connect at night through sleep.

But it is a two-way spiritual threshold. We are in turn also supported by those who have crossed: "We develop the right feelings toward the dead if we become aware that their spiritual gaze—if I may use that expression—and their powers focus on us; they look at us, act in us, and add to our strength" (Steiner, 1990, p. 57). But this connection is steeped in mutuality:

> To experience such a spiritual fact in the right way, we need to develop a very specific type of selflessness and a capacity for love. That is why I stressed that one could love the person objectively, as it were, because of her qualities; one had to love her because she was as she was. A subjective love, a love arising out of personal needs, can easily be egotistical and can potentially keep us from finding the right relationship to such a dead individual. The difference between the right love, the selfless love we have for such a person, and selfish love becomes perfectly obvious in clairvoyant experience.
>
> Let us assume that such a person would want to help us after her death, but we cannot develop true selfless love for her. Her spiritual gaze, her spiritual will streaming toward us would then be like a burning sensation, causing a piercing, burning feeling in our soul. If we can feel and maintain a selfless love, this stream, her spiritual gaze as it were, flows into our soul like a feeling of warm mildness and pours into our thoughts, imagination, feeling and willing. (ibid., p. 57)

Thus we need to realize that thoughts are living beings. It is possible to break through to those who have departed if our thoughts become accessible to them. They are not interested in the material matters that preoccupy our time on Earth; rather, they want to experience thoughts that move, are alive, and are spiritual.

In previous chapter, I spoke of some of the people in my life who have passed on. Every once in a while I can feel the presence of my Mom or one of the others. Recently, it was William Ward, while attending a delegates' meeting of The Association of Waldorf Schools of North America (AWSNA). Why? One can find the answer by observing one's own thinking at the time. While in a particular frame of mind, one works with thoughts that have life, and then the pathways open up. The dead are very interested in us as spiritual beings.

Rather than looking out into the world, as if we were the center of the universe, one has to be willing to turn from observer to the one being observed:

> When we look at things in the physical world we see forms, figures, actions, things...there is an experience of "looking at." We look at mountains, trees, stars.... But looking with the spiritual eye, perceiving clairvoyantly, one learns to see the actual being of the other person. But it is a different kind of perception; rather than looking at, we develop a feeling of being perceived by.... Thus in regard to the first hierarchy, the angels, it is not correct to say "I perceive an angel," but rather we should say "I feel an angel perceiving me." (ibid., p. 55)

This reversal can have many practical benefits for living on the Earth as well. Rather than living with abstract concepts and old ideas, the "turning" described above can help with bringing new impulses and initiatives into the world. Rather than think that I will wake up in the morning and do something new, one who has become susceptible to being perceived has learned to host the feeling; an initiative has found me, an idea has come to me, a realization has dawned in my consciousness, the things in my lab on which I have been working so long have now jumped out at me in a new way. Initiative finds us. It works from the periphery to the self. It is all a matter of how we prepare ourselves to host initiative. That is why I so enjoy reading the biographies of great innovators. Their great ideas find them!

It helps if we work on ideas that can become ideals, for they give us nourishment and can propel us into doing greater things. Many revolutions are about ideas that become ideals. I have often thought back to my history lessons at Bowdoin College and the wonderful presentations given by my advisor and professor par excellence, John Karl. One episode that keeps returning involves the tumultuous years around the French Revolution, a time of very strong ideals. Words such as liberty, fraternity, equality were so strongly experienced that they motivated masses of people in storming the Bastille and later the palace at Versailles. Yet what has continued to occupy my thoughts, even years later, was the sequence of subsequent events, wave upon wave of actions and reactions that ultimately led to the rise of Napoleon, a figure not all associated with the three ideals I mentioned. What happened?

At first there was something very abstract living in those three words: *liberty, fraternity, equality.* They were slogans, but I wonder how much the average person really understood their true meaning. (Of course some had read Voltaire, Rousseau, and other Enlightenment thinkers.) But when an ideal is too abstract, it tends to flow violently into human action; we see that still today in religious extremism. I feel that abstract ideals that are not penetrated, that are not warmed through inner work, tend to fall into physical solutions. As has happened with countless "revolutions" around the world, many people were not ready to deal with the implications of their ideals. So for example, a full penetration of the ideals of the French Revolution would have led people to realizations along the lines of a possible threefold social order, later to be developed by Rudolf Steiner. When ideals are not lived, they can come back to "reproach" us, and we are challenged to give it another try in a subsequent situation.

Yet when ideals lead to new insights that work into our feeling life, transforming our inner working, then they can become potent forces for change in the world. We see this living in examples of Camphill communities, biodynamic farms and Waldorf schools. These accomplishments are examples of ideals that have been lived and transformed into service to humanity.

These considerations of ideas help us understand why many recommend reading to the dead. This allows us to build a relationship to the departed even while some of us remain on the Earth. But the content of what we read and what we carry into sleep with us each night matters ever so much:

> If the dead draw nourishment from the content of our souls in sleep, then every thought that enters the spiritual world and is concerned with it and its beings, can be perceived by the dead. On the other hand, if we do not cultivate such thoughts, the dead are deprived of them. Ideas related only to the material world, to things in nature, live in our souls in such a way that the dead cannot perceive them. These ideas, however scholarly or wise, are meaningless for the dead. As soon as we have thoughts about the spiritual world, not only the

> living but also the dead, have immediate access to them. That is why we have often recommended that our friends read silently to an individual with whom they were closely connected and who has passed on to the spiritual world. One forms an image of the person and then, while thinking about him or her, one reads on a subject related to the spiritual world. The dead can then participate in the process, which is important. Although the dead are in the world, we know from spiritual science, thoughts about the spiritual world must be produced on Earth. The dead must perceive more than the spiritual world around them; they need the thoughts of those who live on Earth, thoughts that for them are like perceptions.
>
> Most important, and the most beautiful thing we can give the dead, is to read to them in a way I have just described. We can give something to the dead by reading on a spiritual subject.... Thus, although the deceased is in the spiritual world, thoughts from Earth have to flow to him. Illuminating thoughts must flow up to those regions where the dead dwell just as rain streams down from the clouds as a blessing in the physical world. (Steiner, 1990, pp. 40–41)

Spiritual thoughts of those still on the Earth, when carried into sleep, nourish the dead:

> For some time after death, the dead derive their nourishment from the ideas and the unconscious emotions that we here on Earth take into sleep with us. Those who have died perceive a tremendous difference between people who in their waking life are filled only with materialistic feelings and ideas and also take them into sleep, and others who are wholly filled with spiritual ideas while awake and who continue to be filled with them in sleep. The two types of people are as different in their effect on the dead as a barren region where no food can grow, where people would starve, and a fruitful area that offers nourishment in abundance. For many years after death, the dead draw a vitality from the souls sleeping here on Earth filled with spiritual content, a vitality that is similar, only transposed into the spiritual realm, to what we draw in our physical life from the beings of the kingdoms of nature below us. We literally turn ourselves into fruitful pastures for the dead when we fill ourselves with the ideas of spiritual science. (ibid., p. 39)

The dead can become guardian spirits supporting us for our remaining tasks in life. We can attune our soul to gradually feel the presence of the dead as supporting us in our tasks, guiding and protecting us.

> We gradually come to know that the dead do not really die, but merely move to another place. They still participate in what we do. This insight will be more than a vague feeling for us; we will gradually learn to point to the areas where they are active. We will learn to feel them with us when we need forces we cannot find on the physical plane, when we need support from the higher regions. (ibid., pp. 24–25)

We can aid this whole process by consciously picturing a departed person in our mind's eye. For me, this often means holding an image of the person at a characteristic moment in time when the true personality was able to shine through. For example, I can picture Henry Barnes teaching history in my class at Adelphi University; I can see his face, rosy and lively, his bushy eyebrows, his rounded gestures, his modulated voice...I later heard him lecture many times, and his passion for history and his depth of understanding of how Anthroposophy can solve many life riddles lives within me as fresh as ever. Then there was a moment when I attended a meeting in Chestnut Ridge, New York, as a newly appointed General Secretary of the Anthroposophical Society in America. We were invited to lunch at the Fellowship Community, a home for the aged. A special-needs person I had known since childhood came to greet me and said she had saved a place at the table for me, next to Henry Barnes! He had served as General Secretary for many years, and I felt a kind of transition occurring at that modest dinner table. He passed on a few months later. In the subsequent years, when challenged by the cross-currents of that position, I often turned to him for support. And I almost always felt it! Warm, encouraging, supporting me with a gesture pointed to the future. He was both guiding and protecting me!

Only some time afterward did I read Rudolf Steiner's description of the "recreated image," which can become a real force, an organ of the spiritual world through which the deceased are able to initiate connections and contribute to the shaping of those striving onward on the Earth (ibid., p. 45).

I feel that this is particularly important when striving to stay connected with a child that has passed on. The love and support we would be giving on the earthly plane needs to be devoted to "holding" in a new way. Those who have lost a child speak again and again of the intimacy of a continued connection, a stream of love that breaks down all barriers of space and time.

Some say one also has to let go and not hold on for selfish reasons. This is much more complicated that it sounds. Yes, there is something that happens with the passage of time, but the relationship does not dissolve, it evolves. Those I have interviewed for this project have an inwardness of soul and a depth of feeling not often found in people these days. Even when there are few words, those left behind are filled with a living reality that never departs.

13

Conclusion

As I was eating dinner with family in El Paso recently, a fierce late-summer storm broke overhead. Dramatic thunder and lightning was accompanied by a much-needed downpour as we sat at the table with our enchiladas, beans and salad. My two-year-old grandson, Alexander, was distracted by the storm and wanted to go outside. When it finally subsided enough to do so, we ran out front to find a surprise.

Arching from one end of the horizon to the other was a magnificent rainbow! The colors were vivid and yet soft: red, orange, yellow, green, blue, purple gently blending into each other and the gray expanse around them. One end rose from nearby housetops, whereas the other reached across the heavens to nearly touch a distant mountaintop on the other end. Rising faintly from the right side, we could see a double rainbow, visible though more tentative. It arose skyward for a bit and then faded into the clouds.

The adults stood looking up in speechless wonder, as Alexander ran back and forth, splashing in and out of the puddles with his new rubber boots. He did not want to contemplate the miracle in the sky, but was fascinated with dropping pebbles in the flooded waters covering the sidewalk. His innocent play was a world unto itself, connected with us but very much focused on the discovery of earthly wonders.

When we returned inside, I immediately sent some photos to Karine, who was still traveling with Ionas in Europe (visiting music colleges and practicing French!). She wrote back with the timely reminder that "The rainbow bridge is the only visible imagination of the human soul, spanning heavens and the Earth. The Egyptians wore an amulet, or scarab, and on the back was inscribed: 'I am a child of the Earth and of the starry heavens, but I belong to the starry heavens alone.'"

I took all this into my sleep, and the next morning woke up with the words to write this conclusion.

The journey began with the image of the Egyptian false door and the search to make visible the threshold between life and death. Along the way, the journey included personal reflections, the tragedy of a child's death, grief, stories that can help, and our deep-seated wish to stay connected. We are all children of both the Earth and the starry heavens, but as the Egyptians knew so well, our true home is in the spiritual worlds. Their massive pyramids and temples of higher learning were dedicated to a life after death. And the rainbow bridge unites the two.

The double rainbow gives us a hint of both realities present in each moment of our lives.

My friend Julia Bevins reminded me that for a Tibetan Buddhist, the rainbow is an auspicious symbol. Rainbows are seen when great ceremonies have taken place, on the birth of special personages. When a person dies who has realized the luminous ground of being and stabilized that realization, they may attain the "rainbow body," where their body naturally dissipates into rainbow light at the point of death.

And we know from the esoteric teaching of Rudolf Steiner that when we cross over into the spiritual world at death, the image of the rainbow is the easiest to remember. It allows us most easily to recall the relationship between the spiritual world, where it is becoming light, and the physical sense world we left behind (along with all our earthly capacities for knowledge). The rainbow is a mighty image of hope in a life after death.

So now at the end of this book, I arrived at the real reason for taking up this project. More than ever, I have come to the conviction that *life and death are the great signposts of the human journey*, telling us again and again that there is a vast world beyond our physical sense perceptions. It is that world that inspires much creativity and innovation, from great works of art to the latest technological breakthroughs. It is that world that sustains the human spirit in time of darkness, from the gulag to concentration camps. The continuous quest to overcome racism, inequality and other forms of oppression has again and again sparked extraordinary feats of human courage. The spirit can flash like brilliant strokes of lightning on a summer evening.

Those who have crossed are working with us to overcome narcissism and a fixation on self-centered, material things of the earthly world. There is a great expanse beyond our ordinary consciousness. Those who have passed over the rainbow bridge remind us of this essential fact; they are smiling down on our earnest, heartfelt striving. As seen from above, we form a great chalice of light upholding all that is true, beautiful and good.

Death is but a false door separating those in the heavens from those who lovingly gaze up from below. We are but a double rainbow filling the wide expanse of space and time. Crossing is but a transition.

Appendices

Appendix 1: Verses for the Dead

May love of hearts reach out to love of souls
May warmth of love ray out to Spirit-light
Even so would we draw near to you
Thinking with you Thoughts of Spirit
Feeling in you the Love of Worlds
Consciously at one with you
Willing in silent being.
   (Steiner, 1985, p. 217)

Consider, Friend, When We Together Spoke

Consider, friend, when we together spoke,
Was it not pity that we silence broke
Only to utter empty nothingness?

Thus may two birdlings chatter in their tree
Above a river wandering to sea
With urgent wave to join its boundlessness.

Does there not wake a void within your heart,
That year by year you play no other part
Than just this senseless chatter, friend to friend?

When all the while there flows with powerful might
The stream of spirit wisdom, starry bright,
To the ocean godhead where all waters blend.
  (Christian Morgenstern)

I gaze upon thee
In the spiritual World
In which thou art.
May my love mitigate thy warmth,
May my love mitigate thy cold,

May it reach out to thee and help thee
To find thy way
Through Spirit-darkness
To Spirit-light.
    (Steiner, 1985, p. 211)

Express yourself completely,
then keep quiet.
Be like the forces of nature:
when it rains, there is only rain;
when the clouds pass, the sun shines through.
If you open yourself to the Tao,
you are at one with the Tao
and you can embody it completely.
If you open yourself to insight,
you are at one with insight
and you can use it completely.
If you open yourself to loss,
you are at one with loss
and you can accept it completely.
Open yourself to the Tao,
then trust your natural responses;
and everything will fall into place.
    (Lao Tzu *Tao Te Ching*)

That which is Christ-like in me
Will be crucified
It will suffer and be broken

That which is Christ-like in me
Will rise up
It will love and create
   (Michael Leone)

Into cosmic distances I will carry
My feeling heart—so that it grows warm
In the fire of the holy forces' working;

Into cosmic thoughts I will weave

My own thinking—so that it grows clear
In the light of eternal life-becoming;

Into depths of soul I will sink
Devoted contemplation—so that it grows strong
For human work's true aims.

In the peace of God I strive
Amidst life's battles and cares
To prepare my self for the higher Self;

Aspiring to work in joy-filled peace,
Sensing cosmic being in my own being,
I seek to fulfill my human obligation;

May I thus live in anticipation—
Turned toward my destiny's star—
Which gives me my place in spirit realms.
        (Rudolf Steiner, in Selg, p. 34)

Spirit of his soul, active guardian,
May your wings carry
Our souls' entreating love
To the humans in the spheres entrusted to your care
So that, united with your power,
Our pleas may stream with aid
For the soul they seek in love.
        (ibid., p. 19)

Into the fields of Spirit will I send
The faithful love we found on Earth,
Uniting soul with soul.
And thou wilt find my loving thought
When from the Spirit-lands of light
Thou hither turn thy seeking soul
To find what thou dost seek in me.
        (Steiner, 1985, p. 215)

At the Death of a Child I

And the child's soul
Was lent to us
According to thy Will
Out of spirit worlds.
And the child's soul was led back to Thee
According to Thy will
Into spirit worlds.
           (Rudolf Steiner, in Lewis, p. 4)

At the Death of a Child II

Into you stream light that can grip you
I accompany its rays with the warmth of my love
I think with the best uplifting ideas of my thinking
Upon the stirrings of your heart—
They shall strengthen you
They shall support you.
They shall transfigure you.
I should like to gather my uplifting thoughts
Into your spirit path
So that they may connect
With your spirit-will,
That it find itself in all the heavens
Evermore in its own true being.
           (ibid., p. 5)

The Butterfly

Dear Little Soul,
You had formed such a perfect
Little body....
We cannot know now why it was
Necessary that you leave that beautiful
Form behind on the earth, never to be filled....
But we know and feel your loving interest
Still close around us.
You have brought many people close together
Through your presence, and have taught me
Already more lessons than I could have
Imagined.
More are to come as the days grow....

Five months long you were in your cocoon growing in
Joyful anticipation of your unfolding wings
On your birthday....
What colors would we then meet?
The cocoon is empty
The form is unfilled, yet, your colors are with
Us now and always.
Our hearts have been opened by the rain of
Tears, and we experience your colors now like
a rainbow shining through a break in the gray Clouds.
    (Patricia Bloeden, ibid., p. 2)

Not Flesh of My Flesh

Not flesh of my flesh,
Not bone of my bone
But still miraculously
My own.

Never forget
For a single minute:
You didn't grow under my heart
But in it.
    (Carol Lynn Pearson, ibid., p. 2)

Antiphonal to Wordsworth's
Intimations of Immortality

Our death is but a sleep and a remembering,
The Soul that ascends with us, our life's Cosmos,
Hath had in this place here its setting
And goeth far and far,
Not in the slightest forgetfulness
And in anything else than nakedness
But burgeoning clouds of glory do we go
To God, Who is our Home;
Heavenly vitality streams in us
In our new-found vibrancy.
    (Lewis, p. 3)

Appendix 2: Mistletoe

Of the various exceptions conspiring to wake up the gods through the death of Baldur, the one that bears special significance for our time is the substance of the dart itself, the mistletoe. As a gardener and lover of nature all my life, this particular plant is the most extraordinary I have ever come across.

There are four species of mistletoe that grow in Europe:

> yellow-berried Loranthus (*Loranthus europaeus*)
> dwarf mistletoe (*Arceuthobium oxycedri*)
> red-berried mistletoe (*Viscum cruciatum*)
> white-berried mistletoe (*Viscum album*)

Of the four, it is the white-berried mistletoe that Rudolf Steiner indicated would be helpful in the treatment of cancer (Gorter, p. 10). He gave many indications to Dr. Ita Wegman between 1917 and 1925, with the result that she was able to found the Society for Cancer Research in 1935 with a goal of optimizing mistletoe processing and concentrating efforts on the manufacture, research and development of mistletoe treatment. In 1963 the Lukas Clinic was opened in Arlesheim, Switzerland, a flourishing center that has treated many patients using anthroposophical and conventional medicine.

As one uncovers the characteristics of mistletoe, one finds that there is nothing about this mysterious plant that is normal. As distinct from other plants, it does not grow on the earth, but rather on trees. Instead of roots it has a snake-like feeler with which it anchors itself in the bark of a host tree, thus receiving nourishment (minerals, etc.) from the host tree instead of the earth. But this is only the beginning of the unusual characteristics.

Mistletoe does not grow from below upward, but rather overcomes gravity by spreading its branches in all directions and adopting a spherical shape. Likewise the leaves of the mistletoe develop extremely slowly and only drop off after two to four years—green and hardly withered (Wilkens, p. 22).

Mistletoe grows from April until mid-June and then takes a long pause, resting until Christmas. Only when nature is in its deep sleep of winter does the mistletoe bear fruit, round white berries. Under a transparent skin of each berry is an embryo that is capable of germinating, but not by itself or by usual methods. Only with the help of certain birds can the berries propagate. A mistle thrush can eat ten to twelve berries, swallowing them whole during the winter months. It then sits at the very top of the tree and digests the meal. After a while, the remnants of its digestion, i.e. slimy seeds capable of germinating, drop down. Some will stick to the branch where they may germinate later. In contrast, a blackcap picks a single berry, separates the skin from the seed, swallows the skin and leaves the seed adhering to the branch.

In either case, the slimy, sticky pulp of the fruit dries up, affixing the seed to the host branch. Germination then begins in April as a green shoot emerges from the seed. The tip of it grows toward the tree bark. By the end of May the tip of the young shoot has pushed against the branch and developed an adhesive disk called a hold-fast. Not until August or September does the young plant manage to come upright on its hold-fast. Even though it does not grow any more in autumn and winter, it remains green, with the original seed beginning to shrink. In May of the following year the first leaflets appear while the host branch thickens. This indicates that the host tree has accepted the mistletoe plant (Gorter, p. 17).

If one observes the mistletoe branches as they slowly develop, one is struck by how much they resemble young plant seedlings. The leaves appear to be related more to cotyledons (the first seeding leaves) that higher plants grow rather than the usual foliage leaves of mature plants. It is as if the leaves and branches retain the seed quality, the restrained potentiality of life force.

So to summarize some of the key characteristics described thus far:

- potentiality
- simple curves and a spherical structure
- slow to develop
- minimal "earthly influence"

- nutrients obtained from the vascular system of the host tree
- fruit absorbs much light—white, soft sheath
- passive growth—host tree grows around the haustorium

All of these characteristics point to the laws of the etheric, the life body of potentiality. In contrast to the astral (see my books *Organizational Integrity* and *School Renewal* for more on these terms), which tends to speed things up and supports our frenzied consciousness and multi-tasking lives, the etheric wants us to cultivate simplicity. Plants grow rhythmically over time. The mistletoe grows exceptionally slowly, thus indicating life force held in reserve. It leads a simple, uncomplicated life, drawing nutrients that have already been processed by a host tree. The mistletoe is an antidote to our modern lifestyle.

A mistletoe bush will begin to flower only after five to seven years. I was particularly curious to find that the flowering reaches its peak in February and March, far outside the normal time of year for all other plants growing in similar regions of Europe. The development of the fruit can take up to nine months, reaching maturity late in the autumn. By then the fruit has lost its green color and the berries turn a shimmering white in the winter sunlight.

Inside the fruit, surrounded by translucent, sweetish fruit pulp, the green embryo lives in a gently muted light that takes it through the winter. Without this light the embryo would quickly die (ibid., p. 25).

This gives us yet another clue as to the special nature of the mistletoe. Of the four aspects of the etheric (chemical, life, warmth, light) it is the light ether that tops off, so to speak, the final stage of its development.

It's no wonder then that this mysterious plant has always fascinated humans and features so frequently in the world's myths and legends. The old Greek legend of Asclepius, the god of healing, tells us that illnesses were cured with mistletoe from oaks. In the heroic epic *Aeneid* by Virgil, the Roman poet, mistletoe opens the gate to the underworld and makes it possible for the dead to return from Hades. Thus mistletoe stands symbolically for the victory of life over death.

This symbolism of death and resurrection is found even more clearly in Norse mythology. Baldur, the god of light and beauty, is beloved of all the gods. None of the other gods is his equal in wisdom, purity and compassion, so they want to protect him from acts of violence. The goddess Frigga makes all creatures take an oath not to harm Baldur. When Loki, the crafty one, who hates Baldur, hears about it, he tears off a mistletoe branch, makes an arrow with it and gives it to Baldur's blind brother who, deceived by Loki, shoots the arrow that pierces Baldur's breast. For the Teutons, the death of Baldur was the greatest misfortune ever suffered by the gods and humanity; thus the mistletoe bore the blame for the greatest of all disasters. Perhaps, today, mistletoe can contribute to modern mythology once more as a powerful weapon in the battle against what is currently our greatest destroyer of life and health—cancer.

The Celts also believed that mistletoe possesses special powers. For them mistletoe berries were above all a symbol of fertility, an almighty divine seed, a symbol that, presumably because of the whitish and slimy consistency of its fruit substance, reminded them of sperm. The Celtic priests, the Druids, brewed a magic potion from oak mistletoe, which they cut at certain times with secret religious rites using a golden sickle. This drink conferred fertility, strength and healing on those who took it. The Celts' belief in the magic of mistletoe is described in the *Asterix* comics, when the druid Getafix stirs up his magic potion in order to endow the Gallic people with supernatural powers.

In the Middle Ages many Christians believed that mistletoe had magical powers. They wore crosses and amulets of mistletoe wood or, while praying, let mistletoe rosary beads pass through their fingers.

In Europe, especially in the Scandinavian and Anglo-Saxon countries, an old mistletoe custom has been preserved up until now; at Christmas time mistletoe branches are hung on the door to bring good fortune, health, strength and the rich blessings of childhood during the coming year.

In the sphere of healing, the famous physician Paracelsus accepted the ancient recommendation to use mistletoe to treat epilepsy, for which it is still used. In the twelfth century the Christian mystic Hildegard von Bingen used mistletoe to treat sicknesses of the liver, and in 1543 the recommendation to treat abscesses with mistletoe is documented in a book of herbal remedies. Other uses were for alleviating cramp, lowering blood pressure, and folklore advised pregnant women to carry mistletoe on their body in order to ease their confinement later on.

Appendix 3: The Juniper Tree

The Grimm Brothers

It is now long ago, quite two thousand years, since there was a rich man who had a beautiful and pious wife, and they loved each other dearly. They had, however, no children, though they wished for them very much, and the woman prayed for them day and night, but still they had none. Now there was a courtyard in front of their house in which was a juniper tree, and one day in winter the woman was standing beneath it, paring herself an apple, and while she was paring herself the apple she cut her finger, and the blood fell on the snow. "Ah," said the woman, and sighed right heavily, and looked at the blood before her, and was most unhappy, "ah, if I had but a child as red as blood and as white as snow!" And while she thus spoke, she became quite happy in her mind, and felt just as if that were going to happen. Then she went into the house, and a month went by and the snow was gone, and two months, and then everything was green, and then three months, and then all the flowers came out of the earth, and four months, and then all the trees in the wood grew thicker, and the green branches were all closely entwined, and the birds sang until the wood resounded and the blossoms fell from the trees, then the fifth month passed away and she stood under the juniper tree, which smelt so sweetly that her heart leapt, and she fell on her knees and was beside herself with joy, and when the sixth month was over the fruit was large and fine, and then she was quite still, and the seventh month she snatched at the juniper-berries and ate them greedily, then she grew sick and sorrowful, then the eighth month passed, and she called her husband to her, and wept and said, "If I die, then bury me beneath the juniper tree." Then she was quite comfortable and happy until the next month was over, and then she had a child as white as snow and as red as blood, and when she beheld it she was so delighted that she died.

Then her husband buried her beneath the juniper tree, and he began to weep sore; after some time he was more at ease, and though he still wept he could bear it, and after some time longer he took another wife.

By the second wife he had a daughter, but the first wife's child was a little son, and he was red as blood and as white as snow. When the woman looked at her daughter she loved her very much, but then she looked at the little boy and it seemed to cut her to the heart, for the thought came into her mind that he would always stand in her way, and she was forever thinking how she could get all the fortune for her daughter, and the Evil One filled her mind with this till she was quite wroth with the little boy and she pushed him from one corner to the other and slapped him here and cuffed him there, until the poor child was in continual terror, for when he came out of school he had no peace in any place.

One day the woman had gone upstairs to her room, and her little daughter went up, too, and said, "Mother, give me an apple." "Yes, my child," said the woman, and gave her a fine apple out of the chest, but the chest had a great heavy lid with a sharp iron lock. "Mother," said the little daughter, "is brother not to have one too?" This made the woman angry, but she said, "Yes, when he comes out of school." And when she saw from the window that he was coming, it was just as if the Devil entered into her, and she snatched at the apple and took it away again from her daughter, and said, "You shall not have one before your brother." Then she threw the apple into the chest, and shut it. Then the little boy came in at the door, and the Devil made her say to him kindly, "My son, will you have an apple?" and she looked wickedly at him. "Mother," said the little boy, "how dreadful you look! Yes, give me an apple." Then it seemed to her as if she were forced to say to him, "Come with me," and she opened the lid of the chest and said, "Take out an apple for yourself," and while the little boy was stooping inside, the Devil prompted her, and crash! she shut the lid down, and his head flew off and fell among the red apples. Then she was overwhelmed with terror, and thought, *"If I could but make them think it was not done by me!"* So she went upstairs to her room to her chest of drawers, and took a white handkerchief out of the top drawer, and set the head on the neck again, and folded the handkerchief so that nothing could be seen, and she set him on a chair in front of the door, and put the apple in his hand.

After this Marlinchen came into the kitchen to her mother, who was standing by the fire with a pan of hot water before her, which she was constantly stirring around. "Mother," said Marlinchen, "brother is sitting at the door, and he looks quite white, and has an apple in his hand. I asked him to give me the apple, but he did not answer me, and I was quite frightened." "Go back to him," said her mother, "and if he will not answer you, give him a box on the ear." So Marlinchen went to him and said, "Brother, give me the apple." But he was silent, and she gave him a box on the ear, whereupon his head fell off. Marlinchen was terrified, and began crying and screaming, and ran to her mother, and said, "Alas, mother, I have knocked my brother's head off!" And she wept and wept and could not be comforted. "Marlinchen," said the mother, "what have you done? But be quiet and let no one know it; it cannot be helped now, we will make him into black-puddings." Then the mother took the little boy and chopped him in pieces, put him into the pan and made him into black puddings; but Marlinchen stood by weeping and weeping, and all her tears fell into the pan and there was no need of any salt.

Then the father came home, and sat down to dinner and said, "But where is my son?" And the mother served up a great dish of black-puddings, and Marlinchen wept and could not leave off. Then the father again said, "But where is my son?" "Ah," said the mother, "he has gone across the country to his mother's great uncle; he will stay there awhile." "And what is he going to do there? He did not even say goodbye to me."

"Oh, he wanted to go, and asked me if he might stay six weeks, he is well taken care of there." "Ah," said the man, "I feel so unhappy lest all should not be right. He ought to have said goodbye to me." With that he began to eat and said, "Marlinchen, why are you crying? Your brother will certainly come back." Then he said, "Ah, wife, how delicious this food is, give me some more." And the more he ate the more he wanted to have, and he said, "Give me some more, you shall have none of it. It seems to me as if it were all mine." And he ate and ate and threw all the bones under the table, until he had finished the whole. But Marlinchen went away to her chest of drawers, and took her best silk handkerchief out of the bottom drawer, and got all the bones from beneath the table and tied them up in her silk handkerchief, and carried them outside the door, weeping tears of blood. Then she lay down under the juniper tree on the green grass, and after she had lain down there, she suddenly felt light-hearted and did not cry any more. Then the juniper tree began to stir itself, and the branches parted asunder, and moved together again, just as if someone were rejoicing and clapping his hands. At the same time a mist seemed to arise from the tree, and in the centre of this mist it burned like fire, and a beautiful bird flew out of the fire singing magnificently, and he flew high up in the air, and when he was gone, the juniper tree was just as it had been before, and the handkerchief with the bones was no longer there. Marlinchen, however, was as gay and happy as if her brother were still alive. And she went merrily into the house, and sat down to dinner and ate.

But the bird flew away and lighted on a goldsmith's house, and began to sing:

> My mother she killed me,
> My father he ate me,
> My sister, little Marlinchen,
> Gathered together all my bones,
> Tied them in a silken handkerchief,
> Laid them beneath the juniper tree,
> Kywitt, kywitt, what a beautiful bird am I!

The goldsmith was sitting in his workshop making a golden chain, when he heard the bird that was sitting singing on his roof, and very beautiful the song seemed to him. He stood up, but as he crossed the threshold he lost one of his slippers. But he went away right up the middle of the street with one shoe on and one sock; he had his apron on, and in one hand he had the golden chain and in the other the pincers, and the sun was shining brightly on the street. Then he went right on and stood still, and said to the bird, "Bird, how beautifully you sing! Sing me that piece again." "No," said the bird; "I'll not sing it twice for nothing! Give me the golden chain, and then I will sing it again for you." "There," said the goldsmith, "there is the golden chain for you, now sing me that song again." Then the bird came and took the golden chain in his right claw, and went and sat in front of the goldsmith, and sang:

> My mother she killed me,
> My father he ate me,
> My sister, little Marlinchen,
> Gathered together all my bones,
> Tied them in a silken handkerchief,
> Laid them beneath the juniper tree,
> Kywitt, kywitt, what a beautiful bird am I!

Then the bird flew away to the shoemaker, lighted on his roof, and sang:

> My mother she killed me,
> My father he ate me,
> My sister, little Marlinchen,
> Gathered together all my bones,
> Tied them in a silken handkerchief,
> Laid them beneath the juniper tree,
> Kywitt, kywitt, what a beautiful bird am I!

The shoemaker heard that and ran out of doors in his shirt sleeves, and looked up at his roof, and was forced to hold his hand before his eyes lest the sun should blind him. "Bird," said he, "how beautifully you can sing!" Then he called in at his door, "Wife, just come outside, there is a bird, look at that bird, he certainly can sing." Then he called his daughter and children, and apprentices, boys and girls, and they all came up the street and looked at the bird and saw how beautiful it was, and what fine red and green feathers he had, and how like real gold his neck was, and how the eyes in his head shone like stars. "Bird," said the shoemaker, "now sing me that song again." "Nay," said the bird, "I do not sing twice for nothing; you must give me something." "Wife," said the man, "go to the garret, upon the top shelf there stands a pair of red shoes, bring them

Appendices

down." Then the wife went and brought the shoes. "There, bird," said the man, "now sing me that piece again." Then the bird came and took the shoes in his left claw, and flew back on the roof, and sang:

> My mother she killed me,
> My father he ate me,
> My sister, little Marlinchen,
> Gathered together all my bones,
> Tied them in a silken handkerchief,
> Laid them beneath the juniper tree,
> Kywitt, kywitt, what a beautiful bird am I!

And when he had finished his song he flew away. In his right claw he had the chain and in his left the shoes, and he flew far away to a mill, and the mill went *klipp klapp, klipp klapp, klipp klapp,* and in the mill sat twenty miller's men hewing a stone, and cutting, *hick hack, hick hack, hick hack,* and the mill went *klipp klapp, klipp klapp, klipp klapp.* Then the bird went and sat on a lime-tree that stood in front of the mill, and sang:

> My mother she killed me,

Then one of them stopped working,

> My father he ate me,

Then two more stopped working and listened to that,

> My sister, little Marlinchen,

Then four more stopped,

> Gathered together all my bones,
> Tied them in a silken handkerchief,

Now eight only were hewing,

> Laid them beneath....

Now only five,

> the juniper tree,

And now only one,

> Kywitt, kywitt, what a beautiful bird am I!

Then the last stopped also, and heard the last words. "Bird," said he, "how beautifully you sing! Let me, too, hear that. Sing that once more for me."

"Nay," said the bird, "I will not sing twice for nothing. Give me the millstone, and then I will sing it again."

"Yes," said he, "if it belonged to me only, you should have it."

"Yes, said the others, "if he sings again he shall have it." Then the bird came down, and the twenty millers all set to work with a beam and raised the stone up. And the bird stuck his neck through the hole, and put the stone on as if it were a collar, and flew on to the tree again, and sang:

> My mother she killed me,
> My father he ate me,
> My sister, little Marlinchen,
> Gathered together all my bones,
> Tied them in a silken handkerchief,
> Laid them beneath the juniper tree,
> Kywitt, kywitt, what a beautiful bird am I!

And when he had done singing, he spread his wings, and in his right claw he had the chain, and in his left the shoes, and round his neck the millstone, and he flew far away to his father's house.

In the room sat the father, the mother, and Marlinchen at dinner and the father said, "How light-hearted I feel, how happy I am!" "Nay," said the mother, "I feel so uneasy, just as if a heavy storm were coming." Marlinchen, however, sat weeping and weeping, and then came the bird flying, and as it seated itself on the roof the father said, "Ah, I feel so truly happy, and the sun is shining so beautifully outside, I feel just as if I were about to see some old friend again." "Nay," said the woman, "I feel so anxious, my teeth chatter, and I seem to have fire in my veins." And she tore her stays open, but Marlinchen sat in a corner crying, and held her plate before her eyes and cried until it was quite wet. Then the bird sat on the juniper tree, and sang:

> My mother she killed me,

Then the mother stopped her ears, and shut her eyes, and would not see or hear, but there was a roaring in her ears like the most violent storm, and her eyes burnt and flashed like lightning:

> My father he ate me,

"Ah, mother," says the man, "that is a beautiful bird! He sings so splendidly, and the sun shines so warm, and there is a smell just like cinnamon."

> My sister, little Marlinchen,

Then Marlinchen laid her head on her knees and wept without ceasing, but the man said, "I am going out, I must see the bird quite close." "Oh, don't go," said the woman, "I feel as if the whole house were shaking and on fire." But the man went out and looked at the bird:

> Gathered together all my bones,
> Tied them in a silken handkerchief,
> Laid them beneath the juniper tree,
> Kywitt, kywitt, what a beautiful bird am I!

On this the bird let the golden chain fall, and it fell exactly round the man's neck, and so exactly round it that it fitted beautifully. Then he went in and said, "Just look what a fine bird that is, and what a handsome golden chain he has given me, and how pretty he is!" But the woman was terrified, and fell down on the floor in the room, and tore her cap off her head. Then sang the bird once more:

> My mother she killed me,

"Would that I were a thousand feet beneath the earth so as not to hear that!"

> My father he ate me,

Then the woman fell down again as if dead.

> My sister, little Marlinchen,

"Ah, said Marlinchen, "I, too, will go out and see if the bird will give me anything," and she went out.

> Gathered together all my bones,
> Tied them in a silken handkerchief,

Then he threw down the shoes to her.

> Laid them beneath the juniper tree,
> Kywitt, kywitt, what a beautiful bird am I!

Then she was light-hearted and joyous, and she put on the new red shoes, and danced and leaped into the house. "Ah," said she, "I was so sad when I went out and now I am so light-hearted; that is a splendid bird, he has given me a pair of red shoes!" "Well," said the woman, and sprang to her feet and her hair stood up like flames of fire, "I feel as if the world were coming to an end! I, too, will go out and see if my heart feels lighter." And as she went out at the door, crash! the bird threw down the millstone on her head, and she was entirely crushed by it. The father and Marlinchen heard what had happened and went out, and smoke, flames and fire were rising from the place, and when that was over, there stood the little brother, and he took his father and Marlinchen by the hand, and all three were right glad, and they went into the house to dinner, and ate.

Appendix 4: The Odor of Chrysanthemums

D. H. Lawrence

I

The small locomotive engine, Number 4, came clanking, stumbling down from Selston—with seven full waggons. It appeared round the corner with loud threats of speed, but the colt that it startled from among the gorse, which still flickered indistinctly in the raw afternoon, outdistanced it at a canter. A woman, walking up the railway line to Underwood, drew back into the hedge, held her basket aside, and watched the footplate of the engine advancing. The trucks thumped heavily past, one by one, with slow inevitable movement, as she stood insignificantly trapped between the jolting black wagons and the hedge; then they curved away toward the coppice where the withered oak leaves dropped noiselessly, while the birds, pulling at the scarlet hips beside the track, made off into the dusk that had already crept into the spinney. In the open, the smoke from the engine sank and cleaved to the rough grass. The fields were dreary and forsaken, and in the marshy strip that led to the whimsey, a reedy pit-pond, the fowls had already abandoned their run among the alders, to roost in the tarred fowl-house. The pit-bank loomed up beyond the pond, flames like red sores licking its ashy sides, in the afternoon's stagnant light. Just beyond rose the tapering chimneys and the clumsy black head-stocks of Brinsley Colliery. The two wheels were spinning fast up against the sky, and the winding-engine rapped out its little spasms. The miners were being turned up.

The engine whistled as it came into the wide bay of railway lines beside the colliery, where rows of trucks stood in harbour.

Miners, single, trailing and in groups, passed like shadows diverging home. At the edge of the ribbed level of sidings squat a low cottage, three steps down from the cinder track. A large bony vine clutched at the house, as if to claw down the tiled roof. Round the bricked yard grew a few wintry primroses. Beyond, the long garden sloped down to a bush-covered brook course. There were some twiggy apple trees, winter-crack trees, and ragged cabbages. Beside the path hung dishevelled pink chrysanthemums, like pink cloths hung on bushes. A woman came stooping out of the felt-covered fowl-house, half-way down the garden. She closed and padlocked the door, then drew herself erect, having brushed some bits from her white apron.

She was a tall woman of imperious mien, handsome, with definite black eyebrows. Her smooth black hair was parted exactly. For a few moments she stood steadily watching the miners as they passed along the railway; then she turned toward the brook course. Her face was calm and set, her mouth was closed with disillusionment. After a moment she called, "John!" There was no answer. She waited, and then said distinctly,

"Where are you?"

"Here!" replied a child's sulky voice from among the bushes. The woman looked piercingly through the dusk.

"Are you at that brook?" she asked sternly.

For answer the child showed himself before the raspberry-canes that rose like whips. He was a small, sturdy boy of five. He stood quite still, defiantly.

"Oh!" said the mother, conciliated. "I thought you were down at that wet brook—and you remember what I told you—"

The boy did not move or answer.

"Come, come on in," she said more gently, "it's getting dark. There's your grandfather's engine coming down the line!"

The lad advanced slowly, with resentful, taciturn movement. He was dressed in trousers and waistcoat of cloth that was too thick and hard for the size of the garments. They were evidently cut down from a man's clothes.

As they went slowly toward the house he tore at the ragged wisps of chrysanthemums and dropped the petals in handfuls along the path.

"Don't do that—it does look nasty," said his mother. He refrained, and she, suddenly pitiful, broke off a twig with three or four wan flowers and held them against her face. When mother and son reached the yard her hand hesitated, and instead of laying the flower aside, she pushed it in her apron-band. The mother and son stood at the foot of the three steps looking across the bay of lines at the passing home of the miners. The trundle of the small train was imminent. Suddenly the engine loomed past the house and came to a stop opposite the gate.

The engine-driver, a short man with round gray beard, leaned out of the cab high above the woman.

"Have you got a cup of tea?" he said in a cheery, hearty fashion.

It was her father. She went in, saying she would mash. Directly, she returned.

"I didn't come to see you on Sunday," began the little gray-bearded man.

"I didn't expect you," said his daughter.

The engine-driver winced; then, reassuming his cheery, airy manner, he said, "Oh, have you heard then? Well, and what do you think—?"

"I think it is soon enough," she replied.

At her brief censure the little man made an impatient gesture, and said coaxingly, yet with dangerous coldness, "Well, what's a man to do? It's no sort of life for a man of my years, to sit at my own hearth like a stranger. And if I'm going to marry again it may as well be soon as late—what does it matter to anybody?"

The woman did not reply, but turned and went into the house. The man in the engine-cab stood assertive, till she returned with a cup of tea and a piece of bread and butter on a plate. She went up the steps and stood near the footplate of the hissing engine.

"You needn't 'a' brought me bread an' butter," said her father. "But a cup of tea"—he sipped appreciatively—"it's very nice." He sipped for a moment or two, then, "I hear as Walter's got another bout on," he said.

"When hasn't he?" said the woman bitterly.

"I heered tell of him in the 'Lord Nelson' braggin' as he was going to spend that b——afore he went, half a sovereign that was."

"When?" asked the woman.

"A' Sat'day night—I know that's true."

"Very likely," she laughed bitterly. "He gives me twenty-three shillings."

"Aye, it's a nice thing, when a man can do nothing with his money but make a beast of himself!" said the gray-whiskered man. The woman turned her head away. Her father swallowed the last of his tea and handed her the cup.

"Aye," he sighed, wiping his mouth. "It's a settler, it is—"

He put his hand on the lever. The little engine strained and groaned, and the train rumbled toward the crossing. The woman again looked across the metals. Darkness was settling over the spaces of the railway and trucks; the miners, in gray sombre groups, were still passing home. The winding-engine pulsed hurriedly, with brief pauses. Elizabeth Bates looked at the dreary flow of men, then she went indoors. Her husband did not come.

The kitchen was small and full of firelight; red coals piled glowing up the chimney mouth. All the life of the room seemed in the white, warm hearth and the steel fender reflecting the red fire. The cloth was laid for tea; cups glinted in the shadows. At the back, where the lowest stairs protruded into the room, the boy sat struggling with a knife and a piece of whitewood. He was almost hidden in the shadow. It was half-past four. They had but to await the father's coming to begin tea. As the mother watched her son's sullen little struggle with the wood, she saw herself in his silence and pertinacity; she saw the father in her child's indifference to all but himself. She seemed to be occupied by her husband. He had probably gone past his home, slunk past his own door, to drink before he came in, while his dinner spoiled and wasted in waiting. She glanced at the clock, then took the potatoes to strain them in the yard. The garden and fields beyond the brook were closed in uncertain darkness. When she rose with the saucepan, leaving the drain steaming into the night behind her, she saw the yellow lamps were lit along the high road that went up the hill away beyond the space of the railway lines and the field.

Then again she watched the men trooping home, fewer now and fewer.

Indoors the fire was sinking and the room was dark red. The woman put her saucepan on the hob, and set a batter pudding near the mouth of the oven. Then she stood unmoving. Directly, gratefully, came quick young steps to the door. Someone hung on the latch a moment, then a little girl entered and began pulling off her outdoor things, dragging a mass of curls, just ripening from gold to brown, over her eyes with her hat.

Her mother chid her for coming late from school, and said she would have to keep her at home the dark winter days.

"Why, mother, it's hardly a bit dark yet. The lamp's not lighted, and my father's not home."

"No, he isn't. But it's a quarter to five! Did you see anything of him?"

The child became serious. She looked at her mother with large, wistful blue eyes.

"No, mother, I've never seen him. Why? Has he come up an' gone past, to Old Brinsley? He hasn't, mother, 'cos I never saw him."

"He'd watch that," said the mother bitterly, "he'd take care as you didn't see him. But you may depend upon it, he's seated in the 'Prince o' Wales.' He wouldn't be this late."

The girl looked at her mother piteously.

"Let's have our teas, mother, should we?" said she.

The mother called John to table. She opened the door once more and looked out across the darkness of the lines. All was deserted; she could not hear the winding-engines.

"Perhaps," she said to herself, "he's stopped to get some ripping done."

They sat down to tea. John, at the end of the table near the door, was almost lost in the darkness. Their faces were hidden from each other. The girl crouched against the fender slowly moving a thick piece of bread before the fire. The lad, his face a dusky mark on the shadow, sat watching her who was transfigured in the red glow.

"I do think it's beautiful to look in the fire," said the child.

"Do you?" said her mother. "Why?"

"It's so red, and full of little caves—and it feels so nice, and you can fair smell it."

"It'll want mending directly," replied her mother, "and then if your father comes he'll carry on and say there never is a fire when a man comes home sweating from the pit.—A public-house is always warm enough."

There was silence till the boy said complainingly, "Make haste, our Annie."

"Well, I am doing! I can't make the fire do it no faster, can I?"

"She keeps wafflin' it about so's to make 'er slow," grumbled the boy.

"Don't have such an evil imagination, child," replied the mother.

Soon the room was busy in the darkness with the crisp sound of crunching. The mother ate very little. She drank her tea determinedly, and sat thinking. When she rose her anger was evident in the stern unbending of her head. She looked at the pudding in the fender, and broke out, "It is a scandalous thing as a man can't even come home to his dinner! If it's crozzled up to a cinder I don't see why I should care. Past his very door he goes to get to a public-house, and here I sit with his dinner waiting for him—"

She went out. As she dropped piece after piece of coal on the red fire, the shadows fell on the walls, till the room was almost in total darkness.

"I canna see," grumbled the invisible John. In spite of herself, the mother laughed.

"You know the way to your mouth," she said. She set the dustpan outside the door. When she came again like a shadow on the hearth, the lad repeated, complaining sulkily, "I canna see."

"Good gracious!" cried the mother irritably, "you're as bad as your father if it's a bit dusk!"

Nevertheless she took a paper spill from a sheaf on the mantelpiece and proceeded to light the lamp that hung from the ceiling in the middle of the room. As she reached up, her figure displayed itself just rounding with maternity.

"Oh, mother—!" exclaimed the girl.

"What?" said the woman, suspended in the act of putting the lamp glass over the flame. The copper reflector shone handsomely on her, as she stood with uplifted arm, turning to face her daughter.

"You've got a flower in your apron!" said the child, in a little rapture at this unusual event.

"Goodness me!" exclaimed the woman, relieved. "One would think the house was afire." She replaced the glass and waited a moment before turning up the wick. A pale shadow was seen floating vaguely on the floor.

"Let me smell!" said the child, still rapturously, coming forward and putting her face to her mother's waist.

"Go along, silly!" said the mother, turning up the lamp. The light revealed their suspense so that the woman felt it almost unbearable. Annie was still bending at her waist. Irritably, the mother took the flowers out from her apron-band.

"Oh, mother—don't take them out!" Annie cried, catching her hand and trying to replace the sprig.

"Such nonsense!" said the mother, turning away. The child put the pale chrysanthemums to her lips, murmuring, "Don't they smell beautiful?"

Her mother gave a short laugh.

"No," she said, "not to me. It was chrysanthemums when I married him, and chrysanthemums when you were born, and the first time they ever brought him home drunk, he'd got brown chrysanthemums in his buttonhole."

She looked at the children. Their eyes and their parted lips were wondering. The mother sat rocking in silence for some time. Then she looked at the clock.

"Twenty minutes to six!" In a tone of fine bitter carelessness she continued, "Eh, he'll not come now till they bring him. There he'll stick! But he needn't come rolling in here in his pit-dirt, for I won't wash him. He can lie on the floor—Eh, what a fool I've been, what a fool! And this is what I came here for, to this dirty hole, rats and all, for him to slink past his very door. Twice last week—he's begun now-"

She silenced herself, and rose to clear the table.

While for an hour or more the children played, subduedly intent, fertile of imagination, united in fear of the mother's wrath, and in dread of their father's home-coming, Mrs. Bates sat in her rocking-chair making a 'singlet' of thick cream-colored flannel, which gave a dull wounded sound as she tore off the gray edge. She worked at her sewing with energy, listening to the children, and her anger wearied itself, lay down to rest, opening its eyes from time to time and steadily watching, its ears raised to listen. Sometimes even her anger quailed and shrank, and the mother suspended her sewing, tracing the footsteps that thudded along the sleepers outside; she would lift her head sharply to bid the children 'hush', but she recovered herself in time, and the footsteps went past the gate, and the children were not flung out of their playing world.

But at last Annie sighed, and gave in. She glanced at her waggon of slippers, and loathed the game. She turned plaintively to her mother.

"Mother!"—but she was inarticulate.

John crept out like a frog from under the sofa. His mother glanced up.

"Yes," she said, "just look at those shirt-sleeves!"

The boy held them out to survey them, saying nothing. Then somebody called in a hoarse voice away down the line, and suspense bristled in the room, till two people had gone by outside, talking.

"It is time for bed," said the mother.

"My father hasn't come," wailed Annie plaintively. But her mother was primed with courage.

"Never mind. They'll bring him when he does come—like a log." She meant there would be no scene. "And he may sleep on the floor till he wakes himself. I know he'll not go to work tomorrow after this!"

The children had their hands and faces wiped with a flannel. They were very quiet. When they had put on their nightdresses, they said their prayers, the boy mumbling. The mother looked down at them, at the brown silken bush of intertwining curls in the nape of the girl's neck, at the little black head of the lad, and her heart burst with anger at their father who caused all three such distress. The children hid their faces in her skirts for comfort.

When Mrs Bates came down, the room was strangely empty, with a tension of expectancy. She took up her sewing and stitched for some time without raising her head. Meantime her anger was tinged with fear.

2

The clock struck eight and she rose suddenly, dropping her sewing on her chair. She went to the stairfoot door, opened it, listening. Then she went out, locking the door behind her.

Something scuffled in the yard, and she started, though she knew it was only the rats with which the place was overrun. The night was very dark. In the great bay of railway lines, bulked with trucks, there was no trace of light, only away back she could see a few yellow lamps at the pit-top, and the red smear of the burning pit-bank on the night. She hurried along the edge of the track, then, crossing the converging lines, came to the stile by the white gates, whence she emerged on the road. Then the fear that had led her shrank. People were walking up to New Brinsley; she saw the lights in the houses; twenty yards further on were the broad windows of the "Prince of Wales," very warm and bright, and the loud voices of men could be heard distinctly. What a fool she had been to imagine that anything had happened to him! He was merely drinking over there at the "Prince of Wales." She faltered. She had never yet been to fetch him, and she never would go. So she continued her walk toward the long straggling line of houses, standing blank on the highway. She entered a passage between the dwellings.

"Mr Rigley?—Yes! Did you want him? No, he's not in at this minute."

The raw-boned woman leaned forward from her dark scullery and peered at the other, upon whom fell a dim light through the blind of the kitchen window.

"Is it Mrs Bates?" she asked in a tone tinged with respect.

"Yes. I wondered if your Master was at home. Mine hasn't come yet."

"'Asn't 'e! Oh, Jack's been 'ome an 'ad 'is dinner an' gone out. 'E's just gone for 'alf an hour afore bedtime. Did you call at the 'Prince of Wales'?"

"No—"

"No, you didn't like—! It's not very nice." The other woman was indulgent. There was an awkward pause. "Jack never said nothink about—about your Mester," she said.

"No!—I expect he's stuck in there!"

Elizabeth Bates said this bitterly, and with recklessness. She knew that the woman across the yard was standing at her door listening, but she did not care. As she turned, "Stop a minute! I'll just go an' ask Jack if 'e knows anythink," said Mrs Rigley.

"Oh, no—I wouldn't like to put—!"

"Yes, I will, if you'll just step inside an' see as th' childer doesn't come downstairs and set theirselves afire."

Elizabeth Bates, murmuring a remonstrance, stepped inside. The other woman apologized for the state of the room.

The kitchen needed apology. There were little frocks and trousers and childish undergarments on the squab and on the floor, and a litter of playthings everywhere. On the black American cloth of the table were pieces of bread and cake, crusts, slops, and a teapot with cold tea.

"Eh, ours is just as bad," said Elizabeth Bates, looking at the woman, not at the house. Mrs. Rigley put a shawl over her head and hurried out, saying, "I shanna be a minute."

The other sat, noting with faint disapproval the general untidiness of the room. Then she fell to counting the shoes of various sizes scattered over the floor. There were twelve. She sighed and said to herself, "No wonder!"—glancing at the litter. There came the scratching of two pairs of feet on the yard, and the Rigleys entered. Elizabeth Bates rose. Rigley was a big man, with very large bones. His head looked particularly bony. Across his temple was a blue scar, caused by a wound got in the pit, a wound in which the coal dust remained blue like tattooing.

"Asna 'e come whoam yit?" asked the man, without any form of greeting, but with deference and sympathy. "I couldna say wheer he is—'e's non ower theer!"—he jerked his head to signify the 'Prince of Wales'.

"'E's 'appen gone up to th' 'Yew'," said Mrs. Rigley.

There was another pause. Rigley had evidently something to get off his mind, "Ah left 'im finishin' a stint," he began. "Loose-all 'ad bin gone about ten minutes when we com'n away, an' I shouted, 'Are ter comin,' Walt?' an' 'e said, 'Go on, Ah shanna be but a'ef a minnit,' so we com'n ter th' bottom, me an' Bowers, thinkin' as 'e wor just behind, an' 'ud come up i' th' next bantle—"

He stood perplexed, as if answering a charge of deserting his mate. Elizabeth Bates, now again certain of disaster, hastened to reassure him, "I expect 'e's gone up to th' 'Yew Tree', as you say. It's not the first time. I've fretted myself into a fever before now. He'll come home when they carry him."

"Ay, isn't it too bad!" deplored the other woman.

"I'll just step up to Dick's an' see if 'e IS theer," offered the man, afraid of appearing alarmed, afraid of taking liberties.

"Oh, I wouldn't think of bothering you that far," said Elizabeth Bates, with emphasis, but he knew she was glad of his offer.

As they stumbled up the entry, Elizabeth Bates heard Rigley's wife run across the yard and open her neighbour's door. At this, suddenly all the blood in her body seemed to switch away from her heart.

Appendices

"Mind!" warned Rigley. "Ah've said many a time as Ah'd fill up them ruts in this entry, sumb'dy 'll be breakin' their legs yit."

She recovered herself and walked quickly along with the miner.

"I don't like leaving the children in bed, and nobody in the house," she said.

"No, you dunna!" he replied courteously. They were soon at the gate of the cottage.

"Well, I shanna be many minnits. Dunna you be frettin' now, 'e'll be all right," said the butty.

"Thank you very much, Mr Rigley," she replied.

"You're welcome!" he stammered, moving away. "I shanna be many minnits."

The house was quiet. Elizabeth Bates took off her hat and shawl, and rolled back the rug. When she had finished, she sat down. It was a few minutes past nine. She was startled by the rapid chuff of the winding-engine at the pit, and the sharp whirr of the brakes on the rope as it descended. Again she felt the painful sweep of her blood, and she put her hand to her side, saying aloud, "Good gracious!—it's only the nine o'clock deputy going down," rebuking herself.

She sat still, listening. Half an hour of this, and she was wearied out.

"What am I working myself up like this for?" she said pitiably to herself, "I s'll only be doing myself some damage."

She took out her sewing again.

At a quarter to ten there were footsteps. One person! She watched for the door to open. It was an elderly woman, in a black bonnet and a black woollen shawl—his mother. She was about sixty years old, pale, with blue eyes, and her face all wrinkled and lamentable. She shut the door and turned to her daughter-in-law peevishly.

"Eh, Lizzie, whatever shall we do, whatever shall we do!" she cried.

Elizabeth drew back a little, sharply.

"What is it, mother?" she said.

The elder woman seated herself on the sofa.

"I don't know, child, I can't tell you!"—she shook her head slowly. Elizabeth sat watching her, anxious and vexed.

"I don't know," replied the grandmother, sighing very deeply. "There's no end to my troubles, there isn't. The things I've gone through, I'm sure it's enough—!" She wept without wiping her eyes, the tears running.

"But, mother," interrupted Elizabeth, "what do you mean? What is it?"

The grandmother slowly wiped her eyes. The fountains of her tears were stopped by Elizabeth's directness. She wiped her eyes slowly.

"Poor child! Eh, you poor thing!" she moaned. "I don't know what we're going to do, I don't—and you as you are—it's a thing, it is indeed!"

Elizabeth waited.

"Is he dead?" she asked, and at the words her heart swung violently, though she felt a slight flush of shame at the ultimate extravagance of the question. Her words sufficiently frightened the old lady, almost brought her to herself.

"Don't say so, Elizabeth! We'll hope it's not as bad as that; no, may the Lord spare us that, Elizabeth. Jack Rigley came just as I was sittin' down to a glass afore going to bed, an' 'e said, "Appen you'll go down th' line, Mrs Bates. Walt's had an accident. 'Appen you'll go an' sit wi' 'er 'til we can get him home.' I hadn't time to ask him a word afore he was gone. An' I put my bonnet on an' come straight down, Lizzie. I thought to myself, 'Eh, that poor blessed child, if anybody should come an' tell her of a sudden, there's no knowin' what'll 'appen to 'er.' You mustn't let it upset you, Lizzie—or you know what to expect. How long is it, six months—or is it five, Lizzie? Ay!"—the old woman shook her head—"time slips on, it slips on! Ay!"

Elizabeth's thoughts were busy elsewhere. If he was killed—would she be able to manage on the little pension and what she could earn?—she counted up rapidly. If he was hurt—they wouldn't take him to the hospital—how tiresome he would be to nurse!—but perhaps she'd be able to get him away from the drink and his hateful ways. She would—while he was ill. The tears offered to come to her eyes at the picture. But what sentimental luxury was this she was beginning?—She turned to consider the children. At any rate she was absolutely necessary for them. They were her business.

"Ay!" repeated the old woman, "it seems but a week or two since he brought me his first wages. Ay—he was a good lad, Elizabeth, he was, in his way. I don't know why he got to be such a trouble, I don't. He was a happy lad at home, but full of spirits. But there's no mistake he's been a handful of trouble, he has! I hope the Lord'll spare him to mend his ways. I hope so, I hope so. You've had a sight o' trouble with him, Elizabeth, you have indeed. But he was a jolly enough lad wi' me, he was, I can assure you. I don't know how it is..."

The old woman continued to muse aloud, a monotonous irritating sound, while Elizabeth thought concentratedly, startled once, when she heard the winding-engine chuff quickly, and the brakes skirr with a shriek. Then she heard the engine more slowly, and the brakes made no sound. The old woman did not notice. Elizabeth waited in suspense. The mother-in-law talked, with lapses into silence.

"But he wasn't your son, Lizzie, an' it makes a difference. Whatever he was, I remember him when he was little, an' I learned to understand him and to make allowances. You've got to make allowances for them—"

It was half-past ten, and the old woman was saying, "But it's trouble from beginning to end; you're never too old for trouble, never too old for that—" when the gate banged back, and there were heavy feet on the steps.

"I'll go, Lizzie, let me go," cried the old woman, rising. But Elizabeth was at the door. It was a man in pit-clothes.

"They're bringin' 'im, Missis," he said. Elizabeth's heart halted a moment. Then it surged on again, almost suffocating her.

"Is he—is it bad?" she asked.

The man turned away, looking at the darkness, "The doctor says 'e'd been dead hours. 'E saw 'im i' th' lamp-cabin."

The old woman, who stood just behind Elizabeth, dropped into a chair, and folded her hands, crying, "Oh, my boy, my boy!"

"Hush!" said Elizabeth, with a sharp twitch of a frown. "Be still, mother, don't waken th' children; I wouldn't have them down for anything!"

The old woman moaned softly, rocking herself. The man was drawing away. Elizabeth took a step forward.

"How was it?" she asked.

"Well, I couldn't say for sure," the man replied, very ill at ease. "'E wor finishin' a stint an' th' butties 'ad gone, an' a lot o' stuff come down atop 'n 'im."

"And crushed him?" cried the widow, with a shudder.

"No," said the man, "it fell at th' back of 'im. 'E wor under th' face, an' it niver touched 'im. It shut 'im in. It seems 'e wor smothered."

Elizabeth shrank back. She heard the old woman behind her cry, "What?—what did 'e say it was?"

The man replied, more loudly, "'E wor smothered!"

Then the old woman wailed aloud, and this relieved Elizabeth.

"Oh, mother," she said, putting her hand on the old woman, "don't waken th' children, don't waken th' children."

She wept a little, unknowing, while the old mother rocked herself and moaned. Elizabeth remembered that they were bringing him home, and she must be ready. "They'll lay him in the parlour," she said to herself, standing a moment pale and perplexed.

Then she lighted a candle and went into the tiny room. The air was cold and damp, but she could not make a fire, there was no fireplace. She set down the candle and looked round. The candle-light glittered on the lustre-glasses, on the two vases that held some of the pink chrysanthemums, and on the dark mahogany. There was a cold, deathly smell of chrysanthemums in the room. Elizabeth stood looking at the flowers. She turned away, and calculated whether there would be room to lay him on the floor, between the couch and the chiffonier. She pushed the chairs aside. There would be room to lay him down and to step round him. Then she fetched the old red tablecloth, and another old cloth, spreading them down to save her bit of carpet. She shivered on leaving the parlour; so, from the dresser-drawer she took a clean shirt and put it at the fire to air. All the time her mother-in-law was rocking herself in the chair and moaning.

"You'll have to move from there, mother," said Elizabeth. "They'll be bringing him in. Come in the rocker."

The old mother rose mechanically, and seated herself by the fire, continuing to lament. Elizabeth went into the pantry for another candle, and there, in the little penthouse under the naked tiles, she heard them coming. She stood still in the pantry doorway, listening. She heard them pass the end of the house, and come awkwardly down the three steps, a jumble of shuffling footsteps and muttering voices. The old woman was silent. The men were in the yard.

Then Elizabeth heard Matthews, the manager of the pit, say, "You go in first, Jim. Mind!"

The door came open, and the two women saw a collier backing into the room, holding one end of a stretcher, on which they could see the nailed pit-boots of the dead man. The two carriers halted, the man at the head stooping to the lintel of the door.

"Wheer will you have him?" asked the manager, a short, white-bearded man.

Elizabeth roused herself and came from the pantry carrying the unlighted candle.

"In the parlour," she said.

"In there, Jim!" pointed the manager, and the carriers backed round into the tiny room. The coat with which they had covered the body fell off as they awkwardly turned through the two doorways, and the women saw their man, naked to the waist, lying stripped for work. The old woman began to moan in a low voice of horror.

"Lay th' stretcher at th' side," snapped the manager, "an' put 'im on th' cloths. Mind now, mind! Look you now—!"

One of the men had knocked off a vase of chrysanthemums. He stared awkwardly, then they set down the stretcher. Elizabeth did not look at her husband. As soon as she could get in the room, she went and picked up the broken vase and the flowers.

"Wait a minute!" she said.

The three men waited in silence while she mopped up the water with a duster.

"Eh, what a job, what a job, to be sure!" the manager was saying, rubbing his brow with trouble and perplexity. "Never knew such a thing in my life, never! He'd no business to ha' been left. I never knew such a thing in my life! Fell over him clean as a whistle, an' shut him in. Not four foot of space, there wasn't—yet it scarce bruised him."

He looked down at the dead man, lying prone, half naked, all grimed with coal dust.

"'Sphyxiated,' the doctor said. It IS the most terrible job I've ever known. Seems as if it was done o' purpose. Clean over him, an' shut 'im in, like a mouse-trap"—he made a sharp, descending gesture, with his hand.

The colliers standing by jerked aside their heads in hopeless comment.

The horror of the thing bristled upon them all.

Then they heard the girl's voice upstairs calling shrilly, "Mother, mother—who is it? Mother, who is it?"

Elizabeth hurried to the foot of the stairs and opened the door, "Go to sleep!" she commanded sharply. "What are you shouting about? Go to sleep at once—there's nothing—"

Then she began to mount the stairs. They could hear her on the boards, and on the plaster floor of the little bedroom. They could hear her distinctly, "What's the matter now? What's the matter with you, silly thing?"—her voice was much agitated, with an unreal gentleness.

"I thought it was some men come," said the plaintive voice of the child. "Has he come?"

"Yes, they've brought him. There's nothing to make a fuss about. Go to sleep now, like a good child."

They could hear her voice in the bedroom, they waited whilst she covered the children under the bedclothes.

"Is he drunk?" asked the girl, timidly, faintly.

"No! No—he's not! He—he's asleep."

"Is he asleep downstairs?"

"Yes—and don't make a noise."

There was silence for a moment, then the men heard the frightened child again, "What's that noise?"

"It's nothing, I tell you, what are you bothering for?"

The noise was the grandmother moaning. She was oblivious of everything, sitting on her chair rocking and moaning. The manager put his hand on her arm and bade her "Sh—sh!!"

The old woman opened her eyes and looked at him. She was shocked by this interruption, and seemed to wonder.

"What time is it?"—the plaintive thin voice of the child, sinking back unhappily into sleep, asked this last question.

"Ten o'clock," answered the mother more softly. Then she must have bent down and kissed the children.

Matthews beckoned to the men to come away. They put on their caps and took up the stretcher. Stepping over the body, they tiptoed out of the house. None of them spoke till they were far from the wakeful children.

When Elizabeth came down she found her mother alone on the parlour floor, leaning over the dead man, the tears dropping on him.

"We must lay him out," the wife said. She put on the kettle, then returning knelt at the feet, and began to unfasten the knotted leather laces. The room was clammy and dim with only one candle, so that she had to bend her face almost to the floor. At last she got off the heavy boots and put them away.

"You must help me now," she whispered to the old woman. Together they stripped the man.

When they arose, saw him lying in the naïve dignity of death, the women stood arrested in fear and respect. For a few moments they remained still, looking down, the old mother whimpering. Elizabeth felt countermanded. She saw him, how utterly inviolable he lay in himself. She had nothing to do with him. She could not accept it. Stooping, she laid her hand on him, in claim. He was still warm, for the mine was hot where he had died. His mother had his face between her hands, and was murmuring incoherently. The old tears fell in succession as drops from wet leaves; the mother was not weeping, merely her tears flowed. Elizabeth embraced the body of her husband, with cheek and lips. She seemed to be listening, inquiring, trying to get some connection. But she could not. She was driven away. He was impregnable.

She rose, went into the kitchen, where she poured warm water into a bowl, brought soap and flannel and a soft towel.

"I must wash him," she said.

Then the old mother rose stiffly, and watched Elizabeth as she carefully washed his face, carefully brushing the big blond moustache from his mouth with the flannel. She was afraid with a bottomless fear, so she ministered to him. The old woman, jealous, said, "Let me wipe him!"—and she kneeled on the other side drying slowly as Elizabeth washed, her big black bonnet sometimes brushing the dark head of her daughter.

They worked thus in silence for a long time. They never forgot it was death, and the touch of the man's dead body gave them strange emotions, different in each of the women; a great dread possessed them both, the mother felt the lie was given to her womb, she was denied; the wife felt the utter isolation of the human soul, the child within her was a weight apart from her.

At last it was finished. He was a man of handsome body, and his face showed no traces of drink. He was blonde, full-fleshed, with fine limbs. But he was dead.

"Bless him," whispered his mother, looking always at his face, and speaking out of sheer terror. "Dear lad—bless him!" She spoke in a faint, sibilant ecstasy of fear and mother love.

Elizabeth sank down again to the floor, and put her face against his neck, and trembled and shuddered. But she had to draw away again. He was dead, and her living flesh had no place against his. A great dread and weariness held her; she was so unavailing. Her life was gone like this.

"White as milk he is, clear as a twelve-month baby, bless him, the darling!" the old mother murmured to herself. "Not a mark on him, clear and clean and white, beautiful as ever a child was made," she murmured with pride. Elizabeth kept her face hidden.

"He went peaceful, Lizzie—peaceful as sleep. Isn't he beautiful, the lamb? Ay—he must ha' made his peace, Lizzie. 'Appen he made it all right, Lizzie, shut in there. He'd have time. He wouldn't look like this if he hadn't made his peace. The lamb, the dear lamb. Eh, but he had a hearty laugh. I loved to hear it. He had the heartiest laugh, Lizzie, as a lad—"

Elizabeth looked up. The man's mouth was fallen back, slightly open under the cover of the moustache. The eyes, half shut, did not show glazed in the obscurity. Life with its smoky burning gone from him, had left him apart and utterly alien to her. And she knew what a stranger he was to her. In her womb was ice of fear, because of this separate stranger with whom she had been living as one flesh. Was this what it all meant—utter, intact separateness, obscured by heat of living? In dread she turned her face away. The fact was too deadly. There had been nothing between them, and yet they had come together, exchanging their nakedness repeatedly. Each time he had taken her, they had been two isolated beings, far apart as now. He was no more responsible than she. The child was like ice in her womb. For as she looked at the dead man, her mind, cold and detached, said clearly, "Who am I? What have I been doing? I have been fighting a husband who did not exist. HE existed all the time. What wrong have I done? What was that I have been living with? There lies the reality, this man." And her soul died in her for fear; she knew she had never seen him, he had never seen her, they had met in the dark and had fought in the dark, not knowing whom they met nor whom they fought. And now she saw, and turned silent in seeing. For she had been wrong. She had said he was something he was not; she had felt familiar with him. Whereas he was apart all the while, living as she never lived, feeling as she never felt.

In fear and shame she looked at his naked body, that she had known falsely. And he was the father of her children. Her soul was torn from her body and stood apart. She looked at his naked body and was ashamed, as if she had denied it. After all, it was itself. It seemed awful to her. She looked at his face, and she turned her own face to the wall. For his look was other than hers, his way was not her way. She had denied him what he was—she saw it now. She had refused him as himself. And this had been her life, and his life. She was grateful to death, which restored the truth. And she knew she was not dead.

And all the while her heart was bursting with grief and pity for him. What had he suffered? What stretch of horror for this helpless man! She was rigid with agony. She had not been able to help him. He had been cruelly injured, this naked man, this other being, and she could make no reparation. There were the children—but the children belonged to life. This dead man had nothing to do with them. He and she were only channels through which life had flowed to issue in the children. She was a mother—but how awful she knew it now to have been a wife. And he, dead now, how awful he must have felt it to be a husband. She felt that in the next world he would be a stranger to her. If they met there, in the beyond, they would only be ashamed of what had been before. The children had come, for some mysterious reason, out of both of them. But the children did not unite them. Now he was dead, she knew how eternally he was apart from her, how eternally he had nothing more to do with her. She saw this episode of her life closed. They had denied each other in life. Now he had withdrawn. An anguish came over her. It was finished then; it had become hopeless between them long before he died. Yet he had been her husband. But how little!

"Have you got his shirt, 'Lizabeth?"

Elizabeth turned without answering, though she strove to weep and behave as her mother-in-law expected. But she could not, she was silenced. She went into the kitchen and returned with the garment.

"It is aired," she said, grasping the cotton shirt here and there to try. She was almost ashamed to handle him; what right had she or anyone to lay hands on him; but her touch was humble on his body. It was hard work to clothe him. He was so heavy and inert. A terrible dread gripped her all the while; that he could be so heavy and utterly inert, unresponsive, apart. The horror of the distance between them was almost too much for her—it was so infinite a gap she must look across.

At last it was finished. They covered him with a sheet and left him lying, with his face bound. And she fastened the door of the little parlor, lest the children should see what was lying there. Then, with peace sunk heavy on her heart, she went about making tidy the kitchen. She knew she submitted to life, which was her immediate master. But from death, her ultimate master, she winced with fear and shame.

Appendix 5: When a World Tragedy Comes into a Child or Teen's World

Kim John Payne, M.Ed and Davina Muse, LMHC

Your children, tweens or teens may encounter others who know more about details of a tragedy in world or regional events than they do, from direct exposure to media or from overhearing adult conversations, or from other children at school or in their friendship groups. In the case of natural disasters children may have had some direct experience but may not easily grasp the scope of things. They may feel overwhelmed by what they are hearing and experiencing.

Younger children may come to you for more information, explanations, clarifications, while older ones may need some gentle prompting to speak about what they have been hearing and seeing...this seeking to understand and integrate may take some time. This is an opportunity for parents and teachers to offer wisdom and loving presence, to meet each child in the way he or she needs to be met. Please consider the age of your child and how any of this information may impact him or her—as their parents you are the best expert on how to protect and strengthen your own children and your family. Regardless of their age one thing is constant—they need our reassurance that most people are good, that even in overwhelming disaster, there are always good people helping others in need. Our loving presence and deep quiet listening may be more helpful than a lot of explanations. Children can, and do, work things out for themselves according to their own abilities, over time, in the warmth and calmness of adult presence.

However, if your child either has not directly experienced or heard about a terrible event or has not taken it in, it may be best to "let it be," knowing that when your child *does* want to speak about this, you will be ready. You may be wondering about your child having heard about this and not speaking about it. For the younger child we encourage you to watch your child's play very carefully. For the tween or teen, usually the signs to watch are more in their behavior and attitude. Both play and behavior may be a guide to what is going on inwardly for your child.

Orientation

Simplicity Parenting has at its core, pathways that give direction for everyday family life. However in moments like these they also provide clear and deep orientation for a child who may be in need of reassuring warmth and security as he or she processes this experience.

Soul Fever

Parents will want to observe their children even more lovingly and carefully than usually, if the children have been exposed to a lot of information about a particular tragedy. Some children may come with difficult questions; others may act out what they can't integrate, in play. As much as possible allow this, so long as it is safe. You will want to adjust your family life—by simplifying—if your child seems stressed or anxious, nervous and soul-fevered.

Behavior

Some children may become a little more challenging to you in terms of their behavior. What they are likely doing is looking for your warm but firm boundaries. It is tempting to "cut them some extra slack" at this time. However, loving boundaries, perhaps a little more gently applied, will help them feel secure, as these boundaries and limits reinforce the way that your family defines itself. Also, a special note about transitions such as bed-to-dressed, home-to-school, or play/hanging out time-to-dinner time.... These can be tricky at the best of times but in potentially anxious days like those that may lie ahead, try giving extra time for transitions. Previewing ahead of time how the transition is going to happen and what you expect may also be helpful.

In General...

For more extroverted children...they may act "out" a little more and push the family envelope. They may be more provocative toward you and siblings. For introverted children...they may go inward and become a little quieter or perhaps get stuck or stubborn.

Filtering Out Adult Concerns

We recommend—urge—that younger children not be exposed to news reporting on screen or radio, or adult conversations about this event. Young children do not really grasp that repeated announcements are about *one* single event. Each time they hear a news report or overhear an unguarded adult conversation, the risk is that it sets off a brain-based "cascade" of fight-or-flight hormones which can significantly delay their healing. While tween and teens can intellectually know that these, often sensationalized, reports are about the same event, the same "amygdala hijack," fight-or-flight response occurs on a deeper level. There is a compelling body of research indicating that kids who watch repeated media images of the tragic events could suffer PTSD-like symptoms very similar to the people who were actually involved in the incident first hand.

What to Filter In...

Alternatively, reach into your store of favorite family stories. Tell the familiar beloved stories of Grandpa or Grandma, or maybe some from when you were little. These old stories are familiar and deeply securing to a child of any age.

The filtering-out mantra applies here more than ever. Before you say anything in front of your child, ask yourself three simple questions:

1. Is it *true?*
2. Is it *kind?*
3. Is it *necessary?*

Unless your instinct gives you a very clear "yes" to each of these questions, chances are it is way better to defer the comment until your child is not present.

For tweens and teens, spend time "hanging out" with them. Simply sitting nearby while they do their homework or listening to music is a subtle but important part of being present and available. The metaphor of taking a break from the turbulent waters of world events and mooring your canoe alongside your tween or teenager on a calmer riverbank of simple and familiar family life, seems to fit here.

Rhythm

It may help to light a candle or do some other simple ritual so that children and teens have the understanding that they are sending out their thoughts or prayers to the people who are suffering. Make sure that bedtimes are especially regular, slow and peaceful, so that children and teens have plenty of deep sleep in which to process what has happened in the day. And finally, consider strengthening the rhythms that you already have in family life. In these kinds of situations familiarity brings security. Rhythm quietly and invisibly says to a child, "There are things I can count on. All is well here in this family."

Scheduling

Kids may need more time with parents, more down time, in the next few days and weeks. If your child seems upset by the tragedy, be prepared to quietly, without explanation, simplify your schedule, in favor of more family down time and togetherness. You are in charge of the security, health and peace of mind of your family! Children of all ages do not easily process emotional upset when they are kept busy. This might seem counterintuitive, but distracting and detouring a child away from upset, risks having them circle back to the source and can bring about a very difficult loop of prolonged feelings of uneasiness and even upset, over time.

Environment

A simple, beautiful, calm bedroom and home will help all kids to play, relax or interact more deeply and to be at peace. Play and time outside in nature can be especially helpful. Try to keep the toys, books, clothes a little more tidy than usual. On a deeper level this helps a child or teen have a sense of orderliness in their world, at just a time when this is needed.

How to respond to questions?

Very simple answers to children's questions, that are truthful without going into detail, may help them best to integrate this difficult experience in a healthy way.

Here are some guidelines that may help in case you find yourself at a loss to begin with.

When speaking...

Be sure to use language and words that you know your child already understands, so that he or she can easily absorb what you say. Speak in your normal familiar voice.

If you are asked a question that you may not be sure about how to answer, give yourself time, "That is a big question, honey. I'll think about that." As the day goes on, assess whether the child still needs an answer. Many questions that children have, tend to come and go, and may not actually need answering by us. Often just speaking the question or comment to you, and knowing you have heard them, is enough for your child. Sometimes they may find their own satisfying answers in play.

A special approach for tweens and teens

If a tween or teen asks why would someone want to do such a horrific thing, or what are all the people who have lost their homes going to do, share in their pain and conundrum, ask them what might be living behind their question and essentially be a big loving heart with ears. Tweens and teens usually want to do something besides keep the hurting in their thoughts and prayers (which can be a good thing to do). It may help them to feel they have agency; that they can contribute something to a hurting world.

Perhaps they can collect a few carefully curated toys or clothes for a family who has lost everything in a fire, or make sandwiches or bag lunches or health care kits for people displaced by flood or fire. Parents can check out what local and international organizations are doing and where families can help. Teens (not young children) are often welcome to participate. Sometimes youth groups from churches have good connections with local organizations that need help. It's up to the parents to help investigate options and determine what would be helpful and not overwhelming for their child. It's good when parents can be there serving as well, to help the teen process. If it is an international disaster it's good to find out how your family can partner with reputable relief organizations.*

What you could say...

"Sometimes—almost never—bad things happen...everyone is very sorry about this...and there are lots of loving people helping those families now."

"It is hard for anyone to understand this...and we can help by sending our loving thoughts/ prayers to those families."

"I wonder, is there something you would like to do, or for us to do as a family?"

For the younger child..."You will understand this better when you are bigger. Right now we can send our loving thoughts to those families. We will light a candle for them this evening..."

Many faith communities are offering guidance to parents and families, based on their own particular belief system. You may want to ask your faith leaders for support if you have questions they could answer.

Please use our blog www.simplicityparenting.com as a forum to share children's questions and responses that seemed to be helpful to them, to help other parents.

---

* Thanks to Jan Bryant, Grief Counselor, for the section on tweens and teens: www.janbryant.ca.

Appendix 6. Bringing Death Home

Carla Beebe Comey, March 2014

Recently a dear friend died unexpectedly and, for the first time in my life, I found myself in the midst of making funeral arrangements. No one had discussed his wishes with him. His wife and daughter had not even thought about having to face his death. Everyone was in shock. The need to meaningfully acknowledge his life and allow time for a healing ritual was evident. It was overwhelming just to comprehend the fact that he was gone, and the grief was all-consuming, but the necessity of making arrangements for his remains also called for making decisions. And these decisions needed to be made immediately. But what were the choices? What part could his family play and what would be left to professionals? Our common experience had been to leave everything to the funeral home, but it was heart-wrenching to think of leaving him in the hands of strangers. There was a deep longing to keep him close. When his wife asked, "What are we going to do with his body?" there seemed to be only one choice, we knew we needed to bring him home and spend three last days with him saying goodbye.

Death is inevitable; we all know we will die one day. Funeral arrangements are made every day by loved ones. Every funeral I can remember from my childhood and young adult life had involved whisking the body away and either I never saw my loved one again, or they were embalmed and prepared for a viewing in such a way that they were hardly recognizable. Once death had occurred, loved ones had no involvement in preparing the body for viewing, burial or cremation. The task of dealing with the loved one's remains was delegated to professionals who carried a stigma of being creepy, ghoulish and somehow predatory. During viewings, relatives and friends would glance quickly and then avert their eyes, preferring to focus on the living people in the room and leave as soon as a socially acceptable length of time had passed. Even a closed casket had an invisible circle of space around it which everyone avoided entering. Family and friends would gather for short periods of time, tell the closest loved ones they were sorry for their loss, and we would all go back home and get on with our lives, some with more grief and a need to adjust their daily lives than others. Our experiences had been ones of creating the greatest possible distance from the physical reality of death.

Even though we avoided getting too close, we all knew that having a loved one's body nearby was an important part of final closure. Throughout our lifetimes we had heard countless stories of families waiting for the return of their loved one's remains from a war, accident or natural disaster. Within days of the 9/11 attacks, the New York Times article, "Without a Body to Cry Over," clearly described the pain families feel at not having their deceased's remains returned to them, and voicing their common cry, "Without a body, how do you mark a death, or, more important, a life?" (Sengupta and Baker).

While having remains returned and laid to rest was acknowledged as critical to the healing process, actually taking part in the physical preparation for burial or cremation was not at all part of our experiences. This had not always been the case in the United States. From the colonial days until the 19th century, the funeral and all the associated duties were performed by family and close friends. Family members washed and wrapped the body in a winding cloth. The body was laid in a coffin the family commissioned from the local carpenter and placed in the parlor of the home (Mitford, p. 148). Family and friends kept watch during the vigil, often for three days to allow time for the exit of the spirit (Slucum and Carlson, p. 60). When it was time for the burial, they carried the coffin from the home to the church and graveyard on foot. They often were the ones who dug the grave (Mitford, p. 148).

The Civil War changed everything on an unimaginable scale. For the first time in U.S. history, the government made provisions for soldiers' remains to be returned from the battlefront. In order that decay could be delayed and bodies could be sent over long distances, embalming was widely practiced for the first time. The technique had been developed by French and Italian scientists in the nineteenth century, but the practice was still considered an exotic revival of an Egyptian custom. When President Lincoln's body was embalmed for the journey from Washington DC to Springfield in 1865, it was considered an unusual practice, but it increased public acceptance of the procedure (Laderman, p. 6; Slucum and Carlson, p. 59).

The funeral industry had a vested interest in convincing the public that embalming was necessary for the proper care of the dead; it insured the need for their services. Embalming was advertised as the modern alternative to keeping the body on ice (Slucum and Carlson, p. 60). Chemical companies and undertakers falsely claimed that it served to disinfect bodies and prevent the spread of disease. Yet in 1880 the practice was still not widely practiced. In an effort to professionalize the trade and increase its popularity, chemical companies then sent out salesmen who gave courses and granted "diplomas." By 1900, the home funeral was still the standard, but embalming in the home before the viewing had become a common practice (Laderman, pp. 15–17).

Soon after the turn of the century, due to a number of social changes, the close relationship between the living and their deceased was gradually severed (ibid., p. 1). Life expectancy began to lengthen dramatically and the experience of death in the family decreased (Boyer, p. 214). The number of hospitals across the country increased and they became the chief place of care for the sick. As a direct result, care for the dying moved out of the family home and doctors took primary control, often painfully separating a patient from loved ones (ibid., p. 3). A third major change was the institution of the funeral home. Funeral directors created a "home" for their "necessary" professional services which was a "confusing space of business, religious activity, corpse-preparation and family living" (ibid., p. 7).

The misdeeds of funeral professionals have been well documented, especially in Jessica Mitford's *American Way of Death*, first published in 1963. The hold they have asserted upon the processes of funerals has caused much pain and frustration for many in their time of grief. They have preyed upon families in times of distress, implying that purchasing anything less than the most expensive casket and the most expensive burial plot in the most lavish funeral park would dishonor the memory of the departed (Mitford). They have taken advantage of the social changes of the 20th century to create a monopoly in the death care industry. They have done everything in their power, including the creation of legislation, to insure that their services are required for "proper" care of the body after death, ensuring the separation between the living and their deceased (Mitford; Slucum and Carlson). Whether due to the funeral industry or our own need as a culture to separate ourselves from death, we had collectively come to believe that we could not care in death for those whom we had cared for in life.

In this climate, how then did we even consider the possibility of bringing home a loved one's body for a home funeral? How was it possible to even ask the question, and how was it we had been able to give voice to an inner need to care for his remains? As baby boomers, we had collectively grown up as part of a generation that instituted change and rebelled against many norms of the day. In the 1980s, a small group of baby boomers began to understand that, similar to the home birth movement, it was also time to bring death home. In the 1990s two women gave voice to a growing number of people who were challenging the cultural norm and caring for their own dead. Jerrigrace Lyons of California founded "Passages" in the early 1990s after her good friend Carolyn Whiting died unexpectedly, and Beth Knox founded "Crossings" in 1995 after her seven-year-old daughter died in a car accident. Both women felt an inner compulsion to care for their deceased loved ones at home, and were inspired to help others who wanted to do the same. These two women were the only prominent names in this new practice until the early 2000s (Slucum and Carlson, pp. 138–141). There has been no agency tracking the growth of the movement, but there are currently home funeral directors available in many states across the nation (*Home Funeral Directory*). A simple Google search on March 29, 2014, for "home funerals" brought up more resources and non-profit organizations that are providing support than could be counted.

However holistic a home funeral might be, however rightful it might be to return to natural ways of engaging with the processes of life and death, in my limited experience, conversation about the process of a home funeral initially ignites a feeling of revulsion and fear. Experience has also proven that the thought of participating in such a ritual was far from the actual experience. Heidi Boucher's documentary, *In the Parlor: The Final Goodbye,* chronicles the experiences of three families that chose to have home funerals. They describe a sense of peace and acceptance they are certain was possible only through this close relationship with caring for their deceased. As an adult, I had experienced just such a home funeral and I could concur with the families in the documentary as well as the claims listed on the Seven Ponds website; they are a more loving way to say goodbye, they allow time for closure, they give you control over decisions, they facilitate bonding amongst loved ones, they reinforce the cycle of life, they promote healing and closure, and they return death care to the traditional and natural.

Admittedly, home funerals are not necessarily practical or possible for everyone. They require commitment and a willingness to take on the tasks of physically caring for the body as well as fulfilling any legal requirements. A team of people is needed to complete these physical tasks and legal requirements; a death certificate must be completed by a doctor or coroner and permits may be needed for transporting the body; care must be taken to prepare the body properly; dry ice must be purchased and changed regularly; it must be decided who will hold the vigil and how it will be held; arrangements must be made for burial or cremation. While a home funeral can be a healing therapeutic experience, it takes much effort on the part of family and friends (Seven Ponds).

A home funeral was presented to my friend's family as an option, along with a commitment to provide the necessary support. The hope was that we would all find healing and strength through the process. His wife immediately sensed this was the path she wanted to take, but reactions from other family members were initially mixed. His brother was frightened by the description of the process and his daughter was terrified at the thought of seeing her father's body. They were frightened at the thought of not embalming and using dry ice to preserve the body. They were terrified at the thought of bringing his body into the home and taking three days and nights to sit with him. But his wife knew she needed this time to say goodbye, and with the strength of her friends and family around her, she made the choice to bring him home.

That night we washed his body, anointed him with oil and dressed him in his favorite clothes. Already on that first evening, hesitant family members drew closer and joined the dressing. We placed him carefully in the casket and held a spontaneous ritual to begin the vigil, thoughts, prayers and blessings offered freely. We spent the next three days and nights talking to him, laughing with him, reading his favorite books. We sang, we prayed, we told stories. Friends from near and far came to say goodbye. We celebrated his life.

Words are inadequate to describe the magnitude of our experience, but suffice it to say, gradually over the days our souls were deeply touched. A new appreciation for the precious nature of life, and gratitude for both the living and the dead grew deep inside each one of us, healing and transforming our grief. Gary Laderman, in *Rest in Peace*, claims that by creating rituals and carefully managing the relationship between the living and the dead, we find our way toward making sense of the chaos of death, but perhaps Max Alexander, in his *Smithsonian* article, "The Surprising Satisfactions of a Home Funeral," said it best: "It occurred to me that if more Americans spent more time with their dead—at least until the next morning—they would come away with a new respect for life, and possibly a larger view of the world."

On the last day, my friend's brother shared that without this experience he never would have believed such profound grief could be transformed into such joy. Yes, he would still deeply miss his brother, but he had been given the time to share a last celebration of his life, and a chance to say goodbye alongside family and friends. And that had made all the difference.

BIBLIOGRAPHY

Alexander, M. (2009). "The Surprising Satisfactions of Home Funeral," *Smithsonian Magazine*. March 2009 (https://www.smithsonianmag.com/arts-culture/the-surprising-satisfactions-of-a-home-funeral-53172008).

Boucher, H. (producer, director). *In the Parlor: The Final Goodbye*. Tiny Octopus Production: http://vimeo.com/43712288.

Boyer, P. (1994). *Religion Explained: The Evolutionary Origins of Religious Thought*. New York: Basic Books.

Crossings (2014). "Preparing the Body for a Home Funeral Offered by Crossings: Caring for Our Own" (http://crossings.net).

Clinton, B., and J. Patterson (2018). *The President is Missing: A Novel*. New York: Penguin.

Dougy Center (1999). *35 Ways to Help a Grieving Child*. Portland OR: Dougy Center for Grieving Children.

Dietzel, M. (2010). *Laughing in a Waterfall*. St. Paul, MN: Laughing Bridge.

Goethe, J. W. (2001). *Faust: A Tragedy*, 2nd ed. (tr. W. Arndt). New York: Norton.

Gorter, R. W., MD (1998). *Iscador: Mistletoe Preparations Used in Anthroposophically Extended Cancer Treatment*. Chestnut Ridge, NY: Mercury Press.

Grimm, J., and W. Grimm (1944). *Grimm's Fairy Tales: Folk-tales Collected by Jacob Grimm and Wilhelm Grimm*, vol. 1. New York: Pantheon.

Guerber, H. A. (1992). *Myths of the Norsemen: From the Eddas and Sagas*. Mineola, NY: Dover.

Faulkner, O. (2015). *The Egyptian Book of the Dead*. San Francisco: Chronicle Books.

Finser, T. (2001). *School Renewal: A Spiritual Journey for Change*. Gr. Barrington, MA: Anthroposophic Press.

——(2007). *Organizational Integrity: How to Apply the Wisdom of the Body to Develop Healthy Organizations*. Gr. Barrington, MA: SteinerBooks.

———(2014). *A Second Classroom: Parent–Teacher Relationships in a Waldorf School.* Gr. Barrington, MA: SteinerBooks.

———(2017). *Education for Nonviolence: The Waldorf Way.* Gr. Barrington, MA: SteinerBooks.

Home Funeral Directory (2014): https://homefuneraldirectory.com.

Imagine: Center for Coping with Loss: https://www.imaginenj.org/grief-education-schools-teachers.

Kagan, A. (2013). *The Afterlife of Billy Fingers: How My Bad-boy Brother Proved to Me There's Life after Death.* Charlottesville, VA: Hampton Roads.

Laderman, G. (2003). *Rest in Peace: a Cultural History of Death and the Funeral Home in Twentieth-Century America.* New York: Oxford University.

Landau, Judith, and Jack Saul (2004). "Facilitating Family and Community Resilience in Response to Major Disaster," in Walsh, F., and M. McGoldrick. *Living beyond Loss,* New York: Norton.

Lashlie, C. (2003). *He'll Be OK: Growing Gorgeous Boys into Good Men.* New York: Harper.

Lewis, R. (2018). *Help for Those Close to Children Who Have Died* (self-published). Sacramento.

Lewis, S. (2013). *Nurturing Healing Love: A Mother's Journey of Hope and Forgiveness.* Carlsbad, CA: Hay House.

Lindholm, D. *Götter-Schicksal Menschen-Werden* (tr. E. Piening and S. Berlin). Rudolf Steiner School library manuscript, Gr. Barrington, MA.

Mitford, J. (1998, 1963). *The American Way of Death Revisited.* New York: Vintage.

OSHO (Bhagwan Shree Rajneesh). (1972). *The Book of Secrets: A Contemporary Approach to 112 Meditations Found in the Vigyan Bhairav Tantra.* Switzerland: OSHO International.

Payne, K. J., and L. M. Ross (2009). *Simplicity Parenting: Using the Extraordinary Power of Less to Raise Calmer, Happier, and More Secure Kids.* New York: Ballantine.

Pfefferbaum, R. L., et al (Jan 28, 2014). *Int J Emerg Mental Health* author manuscript: "The Burden of Disaster: Part II. Applying Interventions Across the Child's Social Ecology."

Schaefer, D., and, C. Lyons (2010). *How Do We Tell the Children? A Step-by-Step Guide for Helping Children and Teens Cope When Someone Dies,* 4th ed. New York: Newmarket.

Selg, P. (2011). *The Path of the Soul after Death: The Community of the Living and the Dead as Witnessed by Rudolf Steiner in his Eulogies and Farewell Addresses.* Great Barrington, MA: SteinerBooks.

Sengupta, S., and A. Baker (2001). "Rites of Grief, without a Body to Cry Over," *New York Times* (http://www.nytimes.com/2001/09/27/nyregion/27MEMO.html).

Seven Ponds (2014). "Is a Home Funeral always a Good Choice?" (http://www.sevenponds.com/after-death/planning-a-home-funeral).

Slocum, J., and L. Carlson (2011). *Final Rights: Reclaiming the American Way of Death.* Hinesburg, VT: Upper Access.

Steiner, R. (1968). *Life between Death and Rebirth.* New York: Anthroposophic Press (CW 140).

———(1981). «*Der Baldur-Mythos und das Karfreitag-Mysterium*» (tr. T. Finser for this volume). Basel: Rudolf Steiner Verlag; from the lecture course *Wege der geistigen Erkenntnis und der Erneureung künstlerischer Weltanschauung* (paths of spiritual knowledge and renewal of the artistic worldview). Basel: Rudolf Steiner Verlag, 1999 (CW 161).

———(1985). *Verses and Meditations.* London: Rudolf Steiner Press.

———(1990). *The Presence of the Dead on the Spiritual Path.* Hudson, NY: Anthroposophic Press (CW 154).

———(1996). *The Foundations of Human Experience.* Hudson, NY: Anthroposophic Press (CW 293).

———(2005). *The Mission of the Folk-Souls in Relation to Teutonic Mythology,* London: Rudolf Steiner Press (CW 121), lect. 9.

———(2006). *Transforming the Soul,* vol. 2. London: Rudolf Steiner Press (CW 59).

Three Initiates (2007). *The Kybalion: A Study of the Hermetic Philosophy of Ancient Egypt and Greece,* Radford, VA: A&D.

Thích Nhất Hạnh. (2002). *No Death, No Fear: Comforting Wisdom for Life.* New York: Penguin.

Trozzi, M., and K. Massimini (1999). *Talking with Children about Loss: Words, Strategies, and Wisdom to Help Children Cope with Death, Divorce, and Other Difficult Times.* New York: Berkley Publishing.

Ward, W. (2008). *Traveling Light: Walking the Cancer Path.* Gr. Barrington, MA: Lindisfarne.

Wilkens, D., and G. Böhm (2010). *Mistletoe Therapy for Cancer: Prevention, Healing, and Treatment* (tr. P. Clemm). Munich: Random House.

A Note from SteinerBooks

SteinerBooks is a 501(c)(3) not-for-profit organization incorporated in New York State since 1928. Its mission is to promote the progress and welfare of humanity and to increase general awareness of Rudolf Steiner (1861–1925), the Austrian-born polymath writer, lecturer, spiritual scientist, philosopher, cosmologist, educator, psychologist, alchemist, ecologist, Christian mystic, and evolutionary theorist. He developed Anthroposophy ("human wisdom") as a path to unite the spiritual in the human being with the spiritual in the universe. To this end, SteinerBooks publishes and distributes books and utilizes other means such as electronic media, conferences, and other activities to make his works available and to explore themes arising from and related to Anthroposophy and the spiritual–scientific movement Rudolf Steiner founded.

- We commission translations of books by Rudolf Steiner not previously published in English, as well as new translations for updated editions.
- Our goal is to make works on Anthroposophy more widely available by publishing and distributing both introductory and advanced works on spiritual research.
- New books are published for both print and digital editions to reach the widest possible readership.
- Recent technology also makes it practical for us to reissue out-of-print works for the next generation in both print and electronic editions.

SteinerBooks/Anthroposophic Press depends on readers for financial support, which is greatly needed, appreciated, and tax-deductible. Consider a donation by check or other means to SteinerBooks, PO Box 58, Hudson, NY 12534. You can also contribute via PayPal at www.steinerbooks.org. For more information about supporting our work or to make a contribution, please send email to friends@steinerbooks.org.

www.ingramcontent.com/pod-product-compliance
Lightning Source LLC
Chambersburg PA
CBHW030859170426
43193CB00009BA/671